CHOSEN BY A HORSE

CHOSEN BY A HORSE

[A MEMOIR]

susan richards

Published by
Soho Press, Inc.
853 Broadway
New York, NY 10003

Library of Congress Cataloging-in-Publication Data

Richards, Susan, 1949–
Chosen by a horse : a memoir / Susan Richards.
p. cm.
ISBN-10: 1-56947-419-2
ISBN-13: 978-1-56947-419-8

1. Horses—New York (State)—Anecdotes. 2. Richards, Susan, 1949–
3. Women horse owners—New York (State)—Anecdotes.
4. Human-animal relationships—New York (State)—Anecdotes. I. Title.

SF301.R53 2006
636.1'001'9—dc22   2005052337

10 9 8 7 6 5 4 3 2 1

This book is dedicated with love to Allie Dorion, and to my niece and nephews: Marguerite, Nate, and Evan Richards, because they fill my heart with joy.

[1]

IT WAS A cold March day and the horse paddock at the SPCA was full of mud. I stood shivering at the fence in the drizzle as my breath billowed gray mist over the top rail. In my hurry to get there I'd left the house without a hat or gloves, grabbing only a windbreaker from its hook above the basement stairs on my way to the garage.

If I had stopped to think, I would have responded as I usually did when hearing a plea for help for animals sick and suffering at the hands of humans: I might have done nothing, or I might have sent a check. But this time when my friend Judy called to tell me the SPCA had just confiscated forty abused horses from a Standardbred farm and needed help housing them, I ran for my jacket and jumped in the car.

I don't know why this time was different, why in an instant I chose to do something I'd previously avoided. I was not accustomed to going to the rescue. Mine was never the face friends saw smiling over them as they woke up in the hospital after surgery. I wasn't the one they called to drive them to get their stitches out or to pick up the results of lab tests or X-rays or anything medical. I had a horror of sickness, my own or anyone else's.

With such an aversion to illness, why was I standing at the fence watching twenty emaciated broodmares with their foals stumble in the mud? Why did I answer that call? Perhaps it was just a knee-jerk reaction to a deep and abiding love of horses, a love passed down to me by my grandmother, a formidable, sometimes cruel woman who had become my guardian when I was five. As always, I cringed when I remembered my grandmother, and at the same time I envied her a now-vanished world full of ocean liners, Pullman cars, and best of all, horses. When I was growing up, there were still carriages and odd bits of harness in the stable at her home in South Carolina, lovely old carriages that hadn't been driven in thirty years. I'd look at them and feel cheated that I hadn't lived in a time when horsepower provided the only means of transportation.

In my grandmother's attic was a trunk full of riding clothes, hers and her mother's: brown leather field boots that laced up the front, handmade in England; wool tweed riding jackets with leather buttons and small tailored waists; linen breeches with leather leg patches; and wide-hipped jodhpurs with fitted calves.

There was also a coachman's heavy wool livery with

silver buttons engraved with an *H* for Hartshorne, my grandmother's maiden name and my middle name. When I was six or seven I'd go through the contents of this trunk, carefully lifting out the brittle fabrics with the frayed edges and the disintegrating linings, and once, one of the coachman's buttons came off in my hand. I turned it over and on the back it said Superior Quality.

I put the button in my pocket, and thirty-five years later it hung on the bulletin board above my desk at home. It's small and round and evokes more images than a feature-length film. One touch and I'm tugged into a world full of horses and carriages circa 1900: traffic jams of horses, horses broken down, horses parked at the curb, horses eating lunch, horses whose coats shine like the waxed paneling of the Knickerbocker Club on Fifth Avenue, and horses as shaggy as schnauzers. A perpetual horse show: every day, everywhere, all the time.

It was my grandmother who had given me my first horse when I was five.

"Her name is Bunty," my grandmother proclaimed, handing me the lead line as she herself marched out of the pasture, leaving me alone with my new pony.

Standing at the other end of the lead, I squinted up at a fat white body slung between two sets of shaggy legs with a tail that swept the ground at one end and dark narrowed eyes under thick lashes at the other. It was like leaving me alone with a chain saw. I knew I was in mortal danger, but I was holding a horse. *My* horse. The best thing that had ever happened to me. I wish I could say I was a natural from the start. That I hoisted myself onto her back and, with a willow twig for a crop, went for a wild gallop around the field. But the truth is, I had no idea what to do. I stood trembling in my pink sundress, staring at the pretty pony until she lunged forward and removed some of the baby fat packed around my upper arm.

It never got much better than that, not with Bunty. I loved her anyway: blindly, doggedly, through years of her biting, kicking, and embarrassing me in horse shows by sitting down and refusing to enter the show ring, or refusing to leave it. Occasionally her foul mood lifted and she was a pleasure to ride, but most of the time she brought me to tears. At ten I was given a Morgan gelding named Alert and was shocked to discover that a horse could be gentle and affectionate. I hadn't realized what a hostage I'd been and, beginning with Alert, developed a lifelong love of Morgans.

Now when I walked into my barn, I walked into time-lessness: the coachman's button evoking the distant past, my childhood, the present—all merged into one panorama of horses. I already owned three horses, and the time I spent with them wrapped around my day like brackets, the same beginning and ending no matter what happened in the middle. I worried, since turning forty, since I'd developed a bad back. What if I got too weak to take care of my three horses, a mare and two geldings? What if I got too stiff, what if I got too old? My next-door neighbor, Henry, had owned twenty-five dairy cows. He loved every single one like a daughter. Sometime in his late seventies he got old. Arthritis twisted his fingers, and emphysema stole his breath. For a year he crawled on his hands and knees from cow to cow to get the milking done. He hid his face behind his swollen hands and wept the day the big cattle trailer came to take away his herd. From time to time I had feared that something similar might happen to me. And yet, I stood, waiting to take on the care of yet another horse, one in desperate need of a home.

A man stood beside me at the fence, an SPCA volunteer named Ted, who had helped confiscate these horses. After I'd signed the necessary papers, agreeing to foster a mare, he'd come outside with me to help find and then herd her into the trailer for the drive to my farm. Ted was hatless and coatless, in blue jeans and a plaid flannel shirt, splattered with mud from his leather work boots to his unshaven chin. His brown ponytail hung dark and wet, coiled between his shoulder blades. Ted wiped at the raindrops gathering on his wire-rimmed glasses, smearing wet lines across thick bifocals. He wore a small gold stud in one ear and when I moved closer to look at the list he had pulled from his back pocket, I smelled nicotine. He traced a thick, nail-bitten index finger down the computer printout and stopped at number ten.

"Here she is." He tapped the paper. "Current Squeeze."

It was a strange way to acquire a horse, sight unseen, by choosing an appealing name off a Seized Merchandise list from the Ulster County Sheriff's Department. The entire situation was strange. I knew nothing about Standardbreds beyond the fact that they were long-bodied, harness-racing horses, sometimes called trotters because they raced at a trot. I wouldn't have known what to look for beyond general good health and a pleasant temperament, neither of which was relevant in this situation. The closest I'd ever come to a Standardbred had been the occasional high-speed glimpse of a brown face looking out the window of a horse trailer as it sped down the thruway on its way to the track with one of the graceful-looking racing carriages called a sulky strapped to the top.

So with nothing but a list of names before me, I had picked the name I thought would be the most fun to shout across a pasture. I'd already started practicing shouting it in my head: *Current Squeeze! Curry! Squeezy!* Names are important to horse people. It was hard to come up with a good one. Even though I'd had horses almost all my life, I'd only had the chance to pick a name once. It had been fifteen years earlier, when I was getting divorced and the lawyers were fighting over who would get the horses. We'd had several horses, including my Morgan mare, Georgia. After a year of haggling, I was awarded custody of Georgia and was then surprised to discover she was pregnant—the result of an unplanned visit from a nearby Morgan stallion. My ex-husband never would have agreed to give me Georgia if he had known I was getting two horses for the price of one. So when a filly was born a few weeks after Georgia had been settled in my new barn, I named the filly Sweet

Revenge. I'd kept Sweet Revenge long enough to saddle break and train, and when she was four, I had given her to a friend's teenage daughter who had become serious enough about riding to warrant having her own horse.

I still had Georgia, who would be eighteen this spring. Along the way I had also acquired Hotshot and Tempo, two quarter horse geldings, both now in their late twenties. These three were my little equine family, perfect in number and temperament. They had worked out the pecking order years ago and everyone knew his or her place. Fur rarely flew, blood spilled even less often, and probably wouldn't have at all except for Georgia, who occasionally picked on Hotshot because she was a mare and that's what mares do. Hotshot let her because he was utterly devoted. I'd never thought of getting a fourth horse, I didn't want a fourth horse. I was forty-three, I lived alone, I had a herniated disc that had prevented me from riding any faster than a walk for the past two years, and I worked five days a week as a social worker. Yet here I was, considering appealing horse names listed on a police roster.

Ted and I squinted toward the paddock into the chaos of twenty large brown mares shivering around the perimeter of the fence with foals glued to their sides. We were trying to locate a brass tag with the number ten on it hanging from the cheek latch of one of the worn-out halters. The mares struggled in the deep mud on swollen joints weakened by malnutrition and untreated racing injuries. Many of the horses had open, weeping sores on their legs and flanks. All wheezed and coughed with respiratory illnesses, and green phlegm oozed from eyes and noses.

Whatever misery they had escaped, there still was more in this overcrowded paddock deep in filth, where it was impossible to distinguish between mud and manure. The well-intentioned SPCA was overwhelmed. There was no barn or shed to shelter the sick horses from the cold and rain. The small stable attached to the paddock had only four stalls and was already filled with horses that had been confiscated before this newly seized group of forty. The SPCA had never intended to house this new group of horses but instead, through radio and television appeals already on the air that morning, hoped to place all of them in foster homes that same day until their fate could be resolved in court. With luck, no horse would spend even one night in this over-crowded paddock.

It was impossible to read the numbers on any of the tags. The herd jostled and huddled together on the other side of the paddock, as far from the two humans standing at the fence as possible. I felt a wave of fresh anger at this aberrant behav-ior, at what caused it. Horses treated humanely don't run from people. I'd never seen domestic horses react to humans this way and here were forty, cowering against the far fence as though we'd come to shoot them.

More SPCA volunteers appeared, two women to help us find Current Squeeze and to herd her and her foal into the horse trailer that was backed up against the open paddock gate. Ted climbed over the paddock fence and joined the two women, who were ankle deep in mud, waving their arms to try to separate horses enough to walk between them to check the tags for number ten. The herd seemed tied together as they moved in tight circles of exhausted panic. In their panic, some fell to their knees, unable to lift their hooves as the mud gripped and sucked them down. A few of the fallen mares groaned as they struggled to their feet, only to be knocked down again by the frantic movements of the herd around them. The high-pitched whinnies of foals momentarily separated from their mothers added to the terror in the paddock. I couldn't bear to watch another minute.

"Never mind about Current Squeeze," I called. "I'll take anyone."

A few minutes later, one of the bay-colored skeletons stumbled up the trailer ramp, followed by a muddy foal. Ted scrambled after them, securing a thick rubber-coated kick chain across the back, and then he lifted the ramp, locking it in place. He took the list of names out of his back pocket again and walked to the front of the trailer, disappearing inside for a minute. When he reemerged, he hopped onto the wheel fender and shouted across the paddock to me.

"Lay Me Down," he called, waving the list. "Her name's Lay Me Down."

If the only criterion for choosing a horse was a name, I'd gotten a loser. Lay Me Down? It wasn't a name, it was part of a prayer children recited before going to sleep at night. In a different context—say, shouted across a pasture—it might even sound a little wanton. *Lay Me Down! Lay Me!* What would the neighbors think? Giving a horse a name like that was almost as bad as not feeding her. You couldn't even get a nickname out of it. But it was too late. Lay Me Down was already in the trailer; this was no time to make a fuss because of a name.

The parking lot was beginning to fill with trailers as more people arrived to pick up horses. The SPCA had its hands full orchestrating this heartwarming but overwhelming response to its broadcasted appeal for help. Right now I had to move to make way for someone else who could load another horse. Timing was crucial. Every horse there was critically ill and needed immediate medical attention, a responsibility anyone fostering one had agreed to assume. This was the part I most dreaded. My medical phobia. Since Georgia had birthed her foal, when there had been strictly routine visits for a healthy horse, I had called in a vet once a year for vaccinations.

"We're all set to go," a thin thirtyish blonde named Laura called over to me as she climbed into the cab of the truck that would pull Lay Me Down's trailer. After seeing the appeal for help on television, Laura had offered the use of her horse trailer. I'd met her for the first time when I was inside signing papers. She couldn't foster a horse herself, she'd explained; she had too many of her own already.

I headed for my car, not at all anxious to leave this hub of support and expertise to begin caring for two sick horses on my own. What was I thinking, taking on two animals I might have to bury in a back field by next week?

I drove around to the entrance gate and waited for Laura's green truck to appear in my rearview mirror. It would take thirty minutes to get home, forty-five if I slowed down for the trailer. As soon as we got there I'd telephone my friend Allie. If anyone could help me to keep the mare and her foal alive, it was Allie.

[2]

WE REACHED MY home and drove back to the pasture.

"Ready?" Laura said, standing at the back of the trailer, waiting to pull the dead bolt that would release the ramp. Lay Me Down and her foal stood quietly together in the trailer, apparently too weak to raise much of a fuss.

"Ready," I nodded, and we pulled out the bolts and let the ramp down slowly, unhooking the kick chain at the same time. Neither horse moved. Either they didn't know the ramp was down or they didn't want to get out. I was holding a lead line hooked to Lay Me Down's halter to help guide her backward. I gave it a gentle tug. No response. Laura walked to the front and peeked through the little door at the front of the trailer, clucking softly to encourage them.

I called Lay Me Down by name and tapped my fingers lightly against her rump.

"She's asleep," Laura reported.

Asleep? I dropped the lead line and walked toward the front, ducking my head to walk through the trailer door, and stood inches away from Lay Me Down. She was a tall horse, sixteen hands—about five foot four at the shoulder. Face to face, my eyes should have been level with her nose. But she had dropped her head so low I could look along the ridge of her mane straight down her back to the top of her tail. She looked like a complicated wire coat hanger draped with a mud-caked brown pelt. Bones protruded everywhere. I watched her ribs heave up and down for a minute and listened to her wheeze. Her eyes were open but droopy, weeping a whitish discharge that streaked the dried mud on her face. The same discharge was coming out of her nose. I knew she had pneumonia and had been started on antibiotics before leaving the SPCA. She couldn't keep her head up because she was too weak.

The foal was four weeks old and seemed healthier. She was the same color as her mother, a bay without markings, and weighed about two hundred and fifty pounds. When she saw me enter the trailer she put her ears flat back and glared. She wore a blue nylon halter that was already too small, cutting into the downy fur that covered her cheekbones. I wondered if she'd let me close enough to remove it. She stood edgy and hostile at her mother's flank, waiting to see what I was going to do.

I felt overwhelmed. I'd never had a horse this sick; Lay Me Down could walk off this trailer and die. Then what? Even though I'd been around horses all my life, I'd never been present when one actually died. And I'd never had to hand raise an orphan foal. Lay Me Down sighed a wheezy sigh and blinked her runny eyes. If she could still stand, as soon as I got her out of this trailer I'd make her a warm bran mash.

I unclipped the lead line from her halter so she wouldn't trip on it and put both hands on her chest, pushing backward. She opened her eyes a little wider and looked at me, then started backing up.

"Good girl," I urged, keeping the pressure on her chest. I ducked under the breast bar (a padded horizontal bar at a horse's chest height that keeps it from going too far forward in a trailer and also provides support when the trailer brakes) and stayed with her as she backed down the ramp. Her foal turned and walked out head first, pausing at the end of the ramp to wait for her mother, her ears flickering back and forth in a jealous fury. Who was I to touch her mother? She waved her head at me at the end of a snaky neck. She would have liked to nip me the first chance she got.

We got to the end of the ramp and stood on flat ground. Lay Me Down sighed again, and I took her by the halter and decided, instead of leaving her at the gate to find her own way to the turnout (a twenty-by-twenty-foot lean-to–like horse shelter in the middle of this three-acre pasture), I'd walk her there myself. In her condition I wasn't sure she'd see it or have the energy to get there if she did. When we walked past the watering trough, I paused and flicked the surface with my fingers to entice her and, sure enough, she lowered her head and drank. I felt a small surge of joy because I thought it meant she trusted me.

The foal pranced ahead of us, carrying her little tail aloft to remind me she was alert to any funny business. She had long skinny legs that looked awkward until she ran, and then they became instruments of pure grace. She circled in front of her mother, never farther than a few yards away, dancing out her protest to my presence. She seemed wild. I doubted she'd ever been handled, save for being fitted with the halter.

When Lay Me Down finished drinking, she let me lead her the rest of the way to the turnout. She discovered the fresh hay and nudged it around with her nose, looking for the sweetest grasses. It was such a horsey thing to do, so normal and reassuring, that I stopped worrying momentarily. The foal slipped into the turnout, keeping her mother's body between us, and with one final glare at me, ducked her head to nurse.

Laura and I stood outside the turnout in the rain, watching the two of them for a few minutes. This was a scene I never tired of, watching a horse eat hay. I found the image soothing, like watching logs burn in the fireplace. There was something warm and mesmerizing about it. Now that Lay Me Down was safe, I was eager to make the bran mash.

Laura was anxious to leave, too, so she could return to the SPCA to help transport more horses. As soon as we said our good-byes, I headed for the house to mix the bran mash. There I mixed two quarts each of grain and wheat bran in a feed bucket, adding boiling water and stirring until it was the consistency of hot oatmeal. The whole house smelled sweet and nutty. I broke a few carrots into the mixture, then covered the bucket with a towel. It would still be warm but cool enough to eat by the time I carried it back to the turnout. I'd start the foal on a quart of high-protein grain mix and see how she did. In all the confusion at the SPCA I had forgotten to ask about feed and had no idea what feed schedule, if any, had been decided on in the few hours the horses had been there.

I headed back to Lay Me Down, feeling guilty walking past my three horses, squeezed together at their pasture fence, a triumvirate of quivering indignation. They held their heads aloft with nostrils flared toward the scent of the intruders who were visible to them in the far pasture, which lay on the other side of a small pond. It was my Morgan, Georgia, who set the tone for this hostile reception. Her arrogance was partly my fault, the result of being raised in a barn where "no" was just a theory.

Because of Lay Me Down's pneumonia, it wasn't safe to pet my three horses until I had changed my clothes and disinfected my hands and boots with bleach. I ducked my head and walked fast, wondering what Georgia would have to say about this later.

Lay Me Down was still eating hay when I arrived with her bran mash, but the foal was asleep in a nest of wood shavings, her long legs sprawled out to one side. I worried about mares stepping on these fragile foal-legs, but Georgia never had, and I imagined Lay Me Down wouldn't either.

The foal woke as soon as I entered the shed and scrambled onto her legs, rear first, so for a moment her butt swayed in the air as she wobbled herself upright. She tossed me one of her nasty looks and gave her mother's side a few rough jabs before she turned and lowered her head to suckle again. I wondered if she would ever like me.

There were two feed bins in the shed, one for an adult horse mounted on the wall too high for the foal to reach and one mounted lower called a creep, which had metal grating over the top that only a foal's slender nose could fit through, preventing the mother from stealing the foal's grain. I poured the bran mash into Lay Me Down's bin and right away the droopy eyes looked up, the ears flickered forward, and Lay Me Down stopped eating hay and came over. She hesitated briefly, letting her nose hover over the warm feed bin, perhaps worried about the strange steam, or perhaps reacquainting herself with the unfamiliar smell of food. But after a moment she lowered her head and began to eat.

I stood near, close enough to touch her if I wanted to, but I didn't. Not yet. I just watched. I was trying to understand who she was, what she was like, and how the way she'd been treated would affect her. So far I felt none of the animosity toward me that I was getting from the foal. If anything, I felt a shyness, as though Lay Me Down was also waiting and wondering.

Meanwhile, the foal trotted in tight circles safely on the other side of her mother, adding little bucks and squeals to her nonstop display of fury, this time because her mother had food and she didn't. I hurried into the storage room at one end of the turnout and returned with a quart of grain. As I poured it into the foal's creep, I felt the slightest puff of air ruffle the hair at my temple and, confused about what it could have been, turned to look for whatever feathery lightness had passed so close to my head. And then I noticed the foal staring at me from the corner of the turnout, bouncing around on those jittery new legs, almost useless until they were flying across a field or aiming a kick at someone's head. Her kick had just missed me. I couldn't believe how fast she'd moved or how close she'd come to my temple. I'd been kicked many times by horses, most of the time by accident, occasionally on purpose, but no horse had ever tried to kick me in the head. I knew this foal needed expert handling before anyone would be safe around her. Until then, all I could do was stay aware of where she was and keep my distance.

I walked out of the shed feeling rejected and cold, soaked to the skin in filthy jeans. When I got to the house I'd take a hot shower, put on warm sweats, heat up some mushroom soup, and call Allie. I was past the pond, walking across the lawn toward the back deck of the house, when I looked up and saw my three horses, still standing at the same spot along the fence, wet and miserable, too.

"Hey, guys," I called in my cheeriest voice, wishing I could explain why I wasn't stopping to visit.

When they realized I wasn't coming, three pairs of ears swung flat back, and my mare snaked her head at me over the fence the same way the foal had earlier. I'd lavished food and attention on strange horses right under her nose and after this unbelievable affront, I walked right past her as if she didn't exist.

When Georgia saw me walk up the stairs to the back deck to go inside the house, in one final gesture of fury, she bared her teeth and, turning on Hotshot, bit him on the flank. It was classic mare mind. If you can't bite the one you hate, then bite the one you're with.

[3]

As SOON AS I got Lay Me Down home and settled, I called Allie, my best friend and horsewoman extraordinaire, and asked her to come over and evaluate Lay Me Down's chances for survival.

"I have two more appointments," Allie said. She was a massage therapist. "It'll be several hours before I can get there."

"I hope she lives that long," I said, flipping through *Veterinary Notes for Horse Owners,* a book filled with graphic photos of running sores, tumors, and other ailments that could afflict a horse. I earmarked the chapter on respiratory diseases and pushed it away to read later.

"She'll live," Allie assured me and hung up.

I had my doubts. Three hours later, Allie walked through the front door carrying a beat-up brown leather doctor's bag. Her body was swallowed inside a dark one-piece canvas coverall from Agway made for an average-sized man, not a five-foot, three-inch slender woman. A single blonde French braid fell over her left shoulder, swinging in midair below an ample breast.

"Want some soup?" I asked, reaching for a bowl and ladling some in without waiting for an answer.

"Is that her?" She pointed through the living-room window to the back pasture, where Lay Me Down was only a dark shadow, standing deep inside the turnout.

"There's a foal, too."

Right away she said, "There's nothing wrong with the foal."

We couldn't even see the foal from the house, and I hadn't told Allie anything about her on the phone earlier, but sometimes Allie just knows things (I suspect that she's a witch). She's a deeply intuitive woman with a gift for healing and "seeing." She sees through touch. Some of the things she sees are spooky, like the time a man came for a massage and as soon as she touched him she saw crying children. Afterward, she did some checking and found out he'd been fired from his teaching position on suspicion of child molestation.

She sees emotional and physical problems, too. If she sees something serious like cancer, she doesn't tell the client, but at the right moment she'll suggest a visit to a doctor. When she sees sadness it's usually a long-standing hurt from childhood—an abusive parent or a family with drinking problems. Sometimes it's just a past where love was in short supply. She sends those people home with salves or essential oils made from flowers and herbs she grows in an organic garden.

Like any good witch, she could have been a doctor. She knows a lot about conventional medicine as well as alternative healing. Her shelves are full of medical books she orders over the Internet with titles I find intimidating and repugnant. However, Allie lugs them to bed for cozy reading and sometimes calls to report on breakthroughs in treatments for diseases I've never heard of. Talking about illness makes me uncomfortable, and I always try to steer the conversation back to safer ground. I laugh when I refer to Allie as my doctor, but the truth is, I'm not really joking and neither are the many others who seek her medical advice.

But all her knowledge of medicine for humans is peanuts compared to what she knows about horses.

While Allie finished her soup, I got up from the counter and opened the basement door around the corner from the kitchen and started pulling barn clothes off the hooks on the wall. Clothes bulged into the stairwell, going halfway down the stairs. There were pants and jackets for every season and every possible weather condition. I had just taken a shower and changed into dry clothes, and now I was going to get wet and dirty all over again. Sometimes this happened three times a day. I put on Gore-Tex everything and walked over to the door by the back deck and stepped into rubber boots.

On the walk, I told Allie what the SPCA had told me about Lay Me Down. She had been born in April of 1980 and had begun training as a trotter for harness racing when she was officially a year old, although she had really been only nine months old. The bylaws of Thoroughbred and Standardbred racing state that all horses turn a year old on January first, regardless of when they were actually born. This meant Lay Me Down was on the track, winning races (making her owner money) at twenty months, even though by racing standards she was legally considered two. This had stressed her still-developing musculoskeletal system, and she was given steroids and other anti-inflammatories to mask injuries and stiffness. This was a practice common in all forms of horse racing. For Lay Me Down, it resulted in permanent, debilitating lameness, ending her racing career by age four. She walked with a pronounced limp in both front legs—a real hobble when she got up until she'd been walking for a few minutes, and she had arthritis in her hocks (elbows) in both rear legs. Looking at her now, it was hard to believe that at the peak of her racing, she was valued at a hundred thousand dollars.

She would have maintained that value as a proven brood-mare, a horse who consistently produced winning off-spring, had she not been starved. During the twelve years she lived as a broodmare, she had been left in an open field with inadequate hay, feed, water, shelter, and veterinary care, yet still managed to produce twelve foals, including the one huddled beside her now. To hide the increasing emaciation of his twenty broodmares, the owner had confined them to a small barn for the past year. Then, for reasons still unknown, he had stopped feeding them altogether.

"The court could issue an order to return them," I told Allie.

"Over my dead body," she said. "We'll steal her first."

Allie had been six when she stole her first horse and got her name in the police beat of the local newspaper. After attending the Dutchess County Fair in Rhinebeck, New York, with her parents, she'd thought the two Shetlands providing pony rides looked overheated and decided to save them. She sneaked back to the fair in the middle of the night (this was in the days before much security) and led the two ponies to the empty garage of nearby weekenders who didn't come up much from the city. There the ponies were free to come and go, grazing on the lush turf of the unmowed backyard, unencumbered by hot, oversized western saddles and squirming children. It seemed to be a perfect rescue until the weekenders appeared and within hours, the ponies were back at their job, shuttling children around the dusty ring.

It was the first of many horse thefts (there were a lot of empty barns back then in Dutchess County, perfect for stashing rescued horses), but after the county fair incident, the police knew which little girl to follow to solve the crime.

A nearby horse vet read about the young horse rustler a year later and offered to channel Allie's zeal by taking her along with him on his farm calls. This was the beginning of what Allie referred to as "medical school." At the same time, neighbors across the street who owned several horses made one available for her to ride. So, between the ages of seven and seventeen, she spent her free time either riding or in "medical school."

At seventeen she left home to work on a large Standardbred racing farm. She started as a groom but quickly rose through the ranks from exercising horses to breaking, training, breeding, and imprinting. By the time she was nineteen, she was managing the entire operation.

Horse racing is a man's world and a difficult arena for any woman to find success in. But Allie made it to the top, first at the Standardbred farm and later managing a Thoroughbred farm. I accused her of owing her success to her looks, because she is a voluptuous Norwegian blonde. And while it's true that men were dazzled by her looks, sooner or later they always recognized her horse expertise. She was a good rider, but her specialty was horse management: training, breeding, and general health care. Even now, fifteen years after having left the horse business to become a massage therapist—a career she felt would be more age friendly—professional barns as well as backyard operations like mine continued to seek her veterinary advice.

We crossed Lay Me Down's pasture (how quickly it had become hers) and stopped under the overhang of the turnout. Allie's doctor's kit rattled to the ground like a bag of dishes. I listened to the rain hitting the roof and watched Allie absorb the sight of the emaciated horse.

"You poor baby." She shook her head and bent to pull a stethoscope out of her bag. She hung it around her neck and walked over to Lay Me Down, who had finished her bran mash and was eating hay again.

"The foal kicks," I warned Allie. As usual, the foal stood on the far side of her mother, but she was eating hay, too, and didn't seem interested in us at the moment. I wondered if she was less cranky because her belly was full, and she felt better.

Allie ran her hands all over Lay Me Down's neck and chest, keeping up a soft chatter. Allie's approach to life was so different from mine. I was standoffish, cautious, an observer. Allie jumped in, fast and fearless: a hugger, a toucher, a player from the first moment. I wasn't sure if she was just petting Lay Me Down or doing something diagnostic. Maybe she was getting Lay Me Down used to her touch so she could listen to her heart and lungs with the stethoscope. Some horses get anxious at the sight of anything pulled out of a bag. Tempo would fix a wild eye on the object, nicker, and trot stiff-legged to a safe distance. But Lay Me Down looked untroubled, her ears fixed forward, a sign of openness, curiosity, trust. She gave Allie a wheezy sniff, leaving wet marks here and there on the dark coveralls Allie wore. Her eyes were intense and quizzical under a slightly furrowed brow.

"What a sweet horse," Allie said, adjusting the stethoscope in her ears, then sliding the little disc under Lay Me Down's ribby middle.

I was beginning to sense the same thing. Everything about Lay Me Down had been easy and obliging, starting with her willingness to get into the trailer at the SPCA, the only horse to "volunteer."

"Her heart's strong," Allie said a few minutes later and moved the stethoscope higher to listen to the lungs. "Oh boy," she said right away.

I immediately tensed, even though I already knew the mare was sick, I already knew she had pneumonia. "She's on antibiotics," I said, hoping to avoid hearing that her lungs might collapse or fill with fluid, that this horse could die at any moment.

"Could be worse," Allie said. She pulled the stethoscope off her neck and folded it back into the bag.

I was so relieved I was willing to listen to any details she wanted to offer. But Allie ignored me as she pulled a thermometer out of her bag and lifted Lay Me Down's tail to insert it. None of my three would have allowed this without being held or tied. Lay Me Down wasn't restrained in any way and chose that moment to close her eyes for a little nap.

Standing by Lay Me Down's rump, Allie got a good look at the foal for the first time. "What a cutie," she said. "She needs a new halter."

I was afraid she'd notice. It meant chasing the foal around a wet pasture, and if we could catch her, wrestling off the old halter and then wrestling her into a new one. Allie and I would surely get roughed up in the process. Two hundred and fifty pounds of kicking, biting horse is a lot to contend with. "I don't think she's been handled at all," I said.

"We'll need a third person then."

I tried to think of all the people who wouldn't mind risking their necks. The list wasn't too long, even among my horsey friends. It might be better to ask someone who didn't know anything about horses, a big strong man who wouldn't think twice about helping with a baby horse. That's what I'd call her, a baby. It sounded so innocent.

Allie pulled out the thermometer, told me Lay Me Down's temperature was slightly elevated, and then talked to me about feed, supplements, and vitamins. We discussed moving her into a stall in the barn, someplace I could completely enclose in order to run a vaporizer to help clear her lungs. It wasn't a bad idea except we both knew it was out of the question. I didn't want to expose my other horses to a sick horse, and even if I had been willing, Lay Me Down was too weak to introduce to an established herd. Even if Lay Me Down had been in perfect health it would have taken a few weeks of controlled introductions before my mare would have allowed another mare in the same pasture. I had seen how ferocious Georgia could be. And then there was the foal.

Thirteen years earlier, a few days before Georgia birthed her own foal, I had moved the geldings (who had been with us for almost a year by then) to the pasture where Lay Me Down was now. After Sweet Revenge was born, I gave mother and foal eight weeks together before reuniting them with the boys. Even then, I divided the communal pasture in half with a single strand of electrified fence wire—boys on one side, mother and foal on the other. Weeks passed. There was much nose sniffing and getting acquainted across the fence, a barrier that was mostly psychological. Yet it allowed Georgia to feel she controlled how close the boys could get to her foal. When it looked like the herd was as reintegrated as possible with the electrified wire still between them, I took the wire down.

It was as though I had allowed men with machine guns into the pasture. The minute that single strand of fencing disappeared, Georgia flew at Hotshot, driving him into a corner, where, it was clear, she intended to kill him. Poor Hotshot was as unprepared for this explosion as I was. He seemed incapable of defending himself against the barrage of hooves and teeth that attacked him from one end of his body to the other. He kept his head low, facing into the corner, trying to let his hindquarters absorb the worst of the blows. Blood spilled, horse hair flew, and into this fray stepped the foal.

I don't know what the foal was thinking, what could have possessed her to decide, at that moment, that the best place to be, in the whole three acres of her world, was in the corner with Hotshot. By then, Georgia was so out of her mind she didn't seem to realize that part of the time she was kicking and biting her own foal. The foal screamed, Hotshot screamed, Georgia screamed, I screamed. I thought it would never end. Probably no more than a minute or two had elapsed since the attack began, but it felt much longer. I ran to that corner, too, and was looking for a way to get close enough to grab someone's halter. Anyone's. Ideally Georgia's. We had a strong relationship. She was my girl, my Georgia peach, my peachums-weechums, my Georgie-Porgie-pooh-bear, my fuzzy-wuzzy-wuzzums. That's how it is when you love a horse. Silly language and sometimes silly beliefs, like hoping my relationship with fuzzy-wuzzy-wuzzums would supersede her instinct to protect her young from the "death threat" cowering in the corner.

When the electrified fence wire pulled loose from the middle rail and wrapped around the foal's neck, I finally sprang into action. I couldn't untangle the foal while Georgia was still in a rage because I'd just get kicked, too, so I grabbed the nearest stick, which was actually a large tree limb, and made a lunge for Hotshot's halter.

"*Move!*" I screamed, pulling him in the direction of the gate, hitting him with the branch to get him to follow me. Hotshot, sweet and dumb, had never been slapped, let alone clubbed. Finally, he moved. My plan was to get him to the gate, open it, let him out, then go back and untangle the foal. And that's more or less what happened.

Within minutes, all four were grazing within a few feet of each other as though nothing had just happened, albeit with Hotshot now on one side of the fence, while the other three were clumped together in the pasture. I could only guess that the reason Georgia perceived Hotshot to be a threat and not Tempo, was because during the get-acquainted phase, when noses were touching across the electric fence, Hotshot showed far more interest in the foal than Tempo had. The foal seemed to return his interest, and the two of them often grazed as near to each other as the fence would permit. My theory was that Georgia was jealous.

Allie and I were still standing in the turnout talking when Judy appeared, the friend who had called to tell me about the SPCA's televised plea for help. Like me, Judy was a social worker and someone who loved horses, though she didn't own any. She had come to see whom I'd brought home and to offer help.

"Well," I said, glancing at Allie, "we could use some help putting a new halter on the foal."

We were three small women in our forties. Allie needed all her fingers to make a living. I had a herniated disc. Judy was just plain out of shape. It was raining. The foal was wild.

"Sure," Judy said.

After disinfecting my hands and boots in a bucket of Clorox and water, I went to the tack room in the barn and found the little leather halter Sweet Revenge had worn when she was a foal. It hung on a wall cluttered with halters and lead lines, bridles and saddles, including the first saddle I'd ever had as a child, a small all-purpose Steuben, as good now, thirty-five years later, as the day it was bought. It flooded me with memories, and I felt old and sad surrounded by the smell of leather and mildew.

The gloom lifted when I heard my three horses trotting

across the field toward the barn. They had seen me and had come to find out what was in it for them. I fished around in the treat bucket and pulled out three alfalfa cubes as steel shoes clattered down the cement center aisle of the barn and stopped outside the tack room. A nose snorted into the space under the door, someone squealed, more clattering as they jostled for position. I opened the door, and Georgia was so close it touched her chest. Her neck arched over me and she gave me one of those utterly surprised looks, eyes big and wide, ears cranked forward. The same look I'd get when I'd find her grazing on the lawn after she had used her rump to knock down a section of fence: *I was minding my own business and suddenly there was this noise behind me and I found myself standing on this really green grass.* I handed out the treats, gave everyone a quick pat, and left while they were still chewing so they wouldn't come after me for more.

Back in the turnout with the new halter, we planned our strategy. We would surround the foal right there, inside the turnout, until one of us could grab her halter while one held her around the rump, and the other, around the chest. Allie was the strongest so she was assigned rump control. I'd go for the chest and Judy, the halter.

Before we budged, the foal sensed something was afoot. She jerked her head up from the hay and flattened her ears. Lay Me Down gave the foal a tired glance and went back to her nap. I handed the new halter to Judy, and the three of us started to walk around the back end of Lay Me

Down toward the foal, who had already positioned herself in the corner.

I sensed our mission was doomed.

As I got closer to the irate foal, I remembered I'd never lost a tooth or broken a bone. I'd never had stitches. My various body parts suddenly seemed precious. I really *like* my knees, I thought. My hands looked good hanging at the end of my arms like that. So what if her halter was a little snug?

I didn't used to be such a chicken. It had gotten worse with age, since my back problems began a few years earlier. I felt so fragile sometimes, so vulnerable. I think it started the first time my back gave out. That day I spent six hours on the kitchen floor, since I couldn't reach the phone for help. My dog came over and lay beside me and, eventually, so did my Siamese cat. My back seized up in the morning, right after I'd come in from barn chores, and I lay on the floor in my smelly clothes until three o'clock in the afternoon when two friends showed up unexpectedly. It could have been worse. Sometimes no one stopped by, and I might be alone in the house for days. I don't think you're ever the same after you've experienced that kind of helplessness, never as confident in your independence. After that, I bought a cell phone and carried it everywhere—I, who hated telephones.

"She doesn't look very friendly," Judy said as the foal bucked herself straight into the air.

"She's just scared, poor thing," Allie cooed, taking a few steps closer. The foal bared her teeth and squealed. Lay Me

Down watched under heavy, bored eyelids. Either she knew her foal could hold her own against the likes of us (this was a no-brainer), or she was tired of mothering this nasty little baby and hoped we were the people from the circus.

Allie continued making reassuring sounds, and we crept closer until we were just out of kicking range. "Now!" At her order, we charged forward: Allie at the rump, Judy at the head, and me at the chest. We had her, all two hundred–plus, squirming, squealing pounds.

Every time the foal bucked, Allie was lifted into the air, but she didn't let go. The foal spun and twirled, and we spun and twirled with her. Judy wasn't holding onto the foal's halter, which was good because we didn't want to injure the foal's neck as she yanked away from us. Judy's job was to stay close enough to the thrashing head to unbuckle the old halter, slip it off, and get the new one on and buckled. As far as I could tell, she hadn't been able to get that close. I had one arm across the foal's chest and the other flung over her back. Her mane was fleecy soft against my face, reminding me that even though she was strong, she was still a baby.

The baby dragged us out of the turnout into the rain. It was as if she knew we didn't have a prayer in our rubber boots once we were on the wet grass that provided perfect traction for her little hooves. They dug into the soft ground and she pulled us around like water skiers. We lost Judy somewhere along the way so I wasn't sure why Allie and I continued to hold on. Perhaps it was because letting go was as tricky as catching her had been. Once we released her, we'd have to get out of the way fast.

We were bounced around and dragged around for a few more minutes, and then I knew I'd had enough.

"I'm going to let go," I yelled to Allie.

"On the count of three," she yelled back.

When she got to three, we both let go. It was like being flung out of a moving car. We landed flat on our backs almost on top of each other. The foal sprang away from us as if she were charging out of the starting gate at Churchill Downs. Her victory lap around the field was breathtaking, full of grace and fury. She ran effortlessly, carrying her head high as though flaunting her victory. We lay where she had ditched us, a little out of breath. Judy appeared and knelt beside us in the wet grass. The drizzle had changed to rain, and it was colder.

"Are you OK?" she asked.

Water trickled inside my collar and down the back of my neck. Bigger drips fell off the ends of hair flattened against my forehead and rolled down my face. They felt like tears, tears about being forty-three and too old to handle horses, tears because everything hurt: my back, my arms, my feelings. I didn't like being dumped, not by a horse, not by anyone. Tears because I was wet and tired and scared. If Lay Me Down died, how would I ever manage to take care of this crazy foal?

The foal bounced to a stop in front of the turnout, tossed a final nicker at us, and disappeared inside. It felt like a slap in the face. At that point I wasn't so much wet as oozing self-pity.

"What an *asshole*," I said.

Allie wiped at the raindrops running into her eyes. "Stop anthropomorphizing," she said, squeezing water out of the end of her braid, "she's not your ex-husband."

[4]

HE NEXT MORNING I was up early and stood at the living-room window barefoot, searching Lay Me Down's pasture. I was relieved to see mother and foal grazing together near the turnout and rushed into jeans, a turtleneck, and an old parka to clean stalls and distribute feed. I made a bran mash for Lay Me Down before I went out and left it cooling by the deck door. I took care of my own three horses first because they'd been waiting for me at the gate ever since they'd seen the light go on in the upstairs bathroom. They knew that once they saw that light it would be about fifteen minutes until I appeared in the pasture with carrots. Much longer than that, and I was asking for a broken fence.

Except for the rare vacation, and once when I had the flu, I hadn't missed a morning feed in fifteen years. I almost couldn't imagine what a leisurely morning would feel like. I allowed myself one hour to do chores and another hour to get ready for work. With Lay Me Down and her foal to care for, I'd need another forty-five minutes.

I didn't mind. Taking care of horses was the best way I could think of to begin a day. Most of the time I felt lucky, as though I was living a way of life that had ended with gas lighting and parasols—the way my grandmother had lived. I was the keeper of a precious legacy, an ancient rite. Until my back episode, I had never considered riding or horse care as physically demanding or even as particularly risky. After that, for the first time I questioned my assumption that I'd have horses forever. That I'd be like my aunt, still riding into her eighties. For the first time, I saw that love alone might not be enough to enable me to keep horses into my dotage.

I reminded myself of all the women I knew who were older than I and who still had horses. Then I checked my pocket for the cell phone and headed for the barn. As soon as I slipped through the fence into the pasture, Georgia flattened her ears and flicked her tail at the geldings to keep them away so she could frisk me for carrots all by herself. She jabbed her nose into my armpits, my neck, my ribs. This was rude horse behavior, and I felt like a bad horse owner for allowing it. Nobody I knew let their horse shove them around the way Georgia shoved me around every morning on my walk to the barn.

She was smart and gregarious and in some ways, more like a dog than a horse. She followed me around (whether or not I had carrots), came when she was called, and changed gaits on voice command (walk, trot, canter, and stop).

She had other endearing qualities. If I was at work and she broke out of the pasture, she'd graze on the lawn for a while, then stand at the end of the driveway and wait for my car. As far as I knew, she'd left the property only once, and that was on a brief visit to my next-door neighbor's bird feeder. She had always had a mind of her own, and before my back gave out, when we were riding miles and miles from home, I'd let her decide the best way to navigate streams or go up and down steep trails.

I didn't like saying no to a horse; humans have restricted equine lives in so many ways. Still, I made a halfhearted attempt to discipline her. I pushed her away and said no a few times—none of which worked very well. What worked best (if there was snow on the ground) was making a snowball and lobbing it at her rump. This signaled the beginning of her favorite game. She'd buck away from me across the pasture, anticipating the next snowball. Snowballs didn't have the same effect on the boys, but the mare's playfulness did, and soon all three would be galloping around me in circles, dodging snowballs.

There was no snow on the ground in March, no snowballs to distract her from my pockets, so we jostled along together until we reached the barn. She stopped just outside the entrance to make sure the boys couldn't get in, while I disappeared inside to prepare feed buckets. Afterward, I broke up a bale of hay and threw it out the hayloft door onto the ground below for the three to share when they were done with their grain.

I decided to forgo grooming because I was anxious to check on Lay Me Down and her foal. As a five-year-old, neglecting to brush daily would have been unthinkable to me, the result of being raised in an atmosphere just this side of a cult. It wasn't a deity we blindly venerated, it was *The Horse*. There were certain rituals and practices that, if not performed daily, had consequences too catastrophic for a child even to imagine. For instance, if you didn't groom your horse twice a day, you were asking for it.

"Mats!" the German riding master who taught at the local stable would scream at some tiny child, flicking the mane of her pony where a small tangle appeared. "*Vut are you tinking?*"

An ungroomed horse was a disgrace, an embarrassment, a sign the owner was bad. It was a clear indication that she was as unprepared for life as she was for riding. She was lazy. She was someone who would never amount to anything and would never fit in. If she didn't brush her horse until her arm ached, its skin might rot, its circulation might stop, it might keel over right there in the stall, too filthy to live. And, worst of all, not brushing her horse would reflect badly on the instructor.

At the very least, not grooming your horse meant you

didn't deserve to own one, and it might be snatched away, given to some more deserving, nameless child who thought nothing of getting up on a December morning to walk to the stable in pitch-black cold to feed and groom before school, and then returning after school to repeat the routine. Failing to do this cheerfully, three hundred and sixty-five days a year, meant something was wrong with you. It meant you didn't have any friends, and your family was mad at you, and there was nowhere on this earth to hide from your shame and wrongness until you went away to college and discovered not everyone in the world was horse obsessed.

I was thirty-three before I had the nerve to skip a grooming. It was a soul-searching decision and I tortured myself all day with what it meant and where it might lead and what would happen to my ungroomed horse and *what if a friend, driving by, noticed the muddy leg from the road?* When nothing too horrible happened, I tried it again, and then again. One thing led to another and, after a while, when I skipped one day, it felt so good, sometimes I skipped a whole week.

When my (ungroomed) horses were done with their grain and were outside, eating hay, I headed over to the other pasture, stopping by the house to pick up the bran mash. Lay Me Down stood under the overhang of her turnout while her foal grazed nearby. I was twenty or thirty feet away when I noticed that Lay Me Down was shivering. Either she was much sicker or it was much colder. I poured the bran mash into her feed bin, put grain in the foal's creep, and ran back to the barn for a thermometer.

While I was there I glanced at the horse blankets hanging in the tack room. None of them would fit Lay Me Down. She was a giant compared to my three, who were at the other end of the horse spectrum. Lay Me Down was taller, longer, wider (even though emaciated), and much broader across the chest. She was shivering, however, so she had to have something.

Right away I knew the only thing that would fit her. I ran to the house and got the king-size quilt off my bed, a one-of-a-kind patchwork quilt of orange-and-yellow-patterned squares, a Marimekko fabric. It had been on my bed for twenty years. As I lugged it across the back lawn to Lay Me Down's pasture, I thought about how I could poke holes in it with a screwdriver and use baling twine to tie it across her chest and secure it under her belly. Not forever, just until I could buy her a coat that fit.

She was still shivering when I returned with the quilt so I let her sniff it for a second before I threw it across her back. She continued eating her bran mash without flinching as the weight of the quilt settled along her spine and the ends fluttered down her sides. It covered her nicely, from her neck to the base of her tail, with plenty of fabric to spread across her chest. I could lace her up like a sneaker. She stood quietly under the quilt, eating, while I punched holes in the front of it with a screwdriver and pulled the twine through. I punched more holes near her belly and threaded the twine underneath her like a girth and hoped that it wouldn't be too itchy.

I didn't know if she'd ever worn a blanket or had anything across her back but a harness, but she seemed unconcerned about the heavy quilt wrapped around her like a hotdog bun. I stood back to look. It wouldn't have been the right moment for some of my fancier horse friends to visit. I started to giggle, then felt terrible to be laughing at this sick, sweet animal who had just let me dress her up like a float in the Rose Bowl Parade.

Her head hung down slightly at the end of her long neck, her ears were up and forward, her runny eyes wide open at me. She had finished her bran mash, and she stood watching me watch her. I wasn't used to a horse who stood so still, who maintained such long stretches of eye contact. Sometimes she sighed one of her wheezy sighs and blinked, but she didn't move away, and she didn't knock me down looking for carrots.

I asked myself the question I asked a lot, as a psychotherapist and as someone who lived with animals, but mostly as someone who grew up in a family with lots of mixed messages. What did her body language say? Sometimes it was easy to read body language, and sometimes I felt like I was doing nothing more than hazarding a wild guess. The rule was, I could make a list of all the things I thought the person (or dog or cat or horse) was saying, but in the end, I had to reduce it to one thing. Just one phrase that conveyed the dominant message.

What was Lay Me Down saying? From the lowered head, the quiet tail, the weight evenly distributed on all four legs, the slow, rhythmic movement of her rib cage as she breathed, I heard, "I'm tired" or "I don't feel well." When I combined the description of her body with her face—eyes looking at me, ears forward, lower lip hanging open slightly—what I heard changed to "I'm curious." If I considered that she stood absolutely still while I carried a large, flapping, bright-colored object toward her across the pasture (all three of mine would have fled at the sight), and then let me tie her up in it, I heard "I trust you." So what was the dominant message? If I added it all up, what I heard was "I like you."

At that exact moment, I got this horse. I understood her nature. It came to me as an image—a cat all dressed up in doll clothes, lying on its back in some little girl's ruffle-trimmed baby carriage, being wheeled around the house. That's who Lay Me Down was. That cat. She was the pet who let you do anything to her, the pet who little boys roughed up and little girls dressed up, and it never bit or scratched or ran away or got mad or did anything but bask in the attention and be a wonderful, affectionate, totally available pet. It was rare in a cat or dog. Such tractability was almost unknown in a horse.

I had never had a docile, loving pet. When I was little and riding in horse shows for children, every once in a while they'd hold something called a gymkhana—a show that combined riding skills with games. The show ring would be set up with little jumps and other obstacles—places you'd have to back out of, a line of poles the rider would weave her pony through, spoon races where competitors carried an egg, potato-sack races where the rider would dismount and get in a sack, pulling her pony behind, and so on.

In the best gymkhana events, horse and rider wore costumes. Not everyone could enter these because it meant you had to have a pony who (like the cat in that baby carriage) had a high tolerance for strange things strapped to its head and costumes that fluttered around its legs. Contestants took these costumes to heart, so they were often elaborate, and at least once in every show, some poor child would end up clinging to a runaway pony whose patience for a petticoat had just expired.

My Shetland pony, Bunty, was a moody creature who tolerated very little. On a bad day she would reject the bridle, the saddle, and the rider. Imagine her reaction to wearing a hat! The single event in which we did well was the potato-sack race, when I stayed on the ground leading her. I hopped as fast as I could, not to win but to stay well ahead of Bunty's teeth.

Lay Me Down would have breezed through a costume event. I was standing in front of the turnout, soaking up her niceness, when I noticed her foal jitterbugging behind me on those flying hooves. I turned and faced the flattened ears, the snaky head, the restless legs, the twitchy tail. Her body language was easy to read. It said, "Go away."

I hated being told to go away. It was a rude, unloving, insensitive thing to say, and I'd heard it all my life, beginning with the people who had raised me and, as an adult, in my marriage. It was the loudest half of the mixed message "I love you, go away." For years, since the end of my marriage, I had made certain I'd never have to hear "Go away" again. My resolve meant changing the kind of people I allowed into my life. No more angry, rejecting, Shetland-pony types.

Yet I could understand why the foal would reject me. It was easy to imagine the kind of treatment she had received or witnessed at the hands of human beings. She had come to a logical conclusion about what to expect from the likes of me. Foals in the wild showed less hostility toward humans than this one exhibited toward me. She'd obviously been hurt. She might have been hit or frightened by rough handling when the halter was fitted. This can frighten foals even when done gently. She would also have witnessed whatever abuse her mother and the rest of the herd had suffered.

For a moment I allowed myself to imagine the origins of the mixed message in my own human family. It wasn't the first time I'd done this, but somehow, right then, in front of the angry foal, the parallels were easier to see and easier to forgive. In my family, one unwanted, unloved generation acted out their unwantedness and unlovability with the next. When my mother died of leukemia, it was as though someone had shattered a glass, sending the shards flying in every direction. Some of the biggest shards disappeared for twenty years. My father vanished into an alcoholic stupor somewhere in another city, and my brother was banished many states away to board at a new school. At age five, I became the ward of a stern grandmother. After

I had lived with her for two years, she decided she was too old to raise me herself, so she sent me to live with strangers, albeit relatives. They remained strangers until the routine of threats and beatings became as familiar as getting tucked into bed at night had once been. Alcoholism was endemic on both sides of the family, fueling the rage that was vented onto the children. Those children, initially victims, later became the next generation of victimizers. This daisy chain of pain didn't end until some in my generation noticed the pattern and decided to put a stop to it, but even then, it required a herculean effort. Watching Lay Me Down and her hostile foal, it was impossible not to connect my own plight with theirs: orphaned, abandoned, mistreated.

I didn't know I was angry until I was about thirty-three. I thought I was just born uncongenial until a therapist suggested I might be reacting to the loss of my parents and being left in the "care" of my grandmother. After that, for years I was nothing *but* angry. I'd get angry if the phone rang. I'd get angry when the clothes dryer buzzed. I'd get angry when the toaster oven went *Ping!* I got so angry at the refrigerator hum I called a repairman. When he arrived and heard the normal sound of a refrigerator, he stood in the kitchen with the tool kit in his hand and, avoiding my glare, advised me simply to unplug it.

Standing near the turnout, thinking about all this, I more or less came to terms with the foal's animosity toward me. What remained troublesome was the physical threat she posed, which meant I had to remain aware of her position whenever I was in her pasture. This time, after glaring at me for a moment, she found her mother's teat under the bulky quilt and began nursing. She had already finished all the grain in her creep. It was a good time to take Lay Me Down's temperature, while she was distracted by the foal. I lifted her tail and inserted a lubricated thermometer.

When I pulled it out three minutes later, I was surprised. No temperature? I slid my hand under the quilt, letting it rest on Lay Me Down's bony flank. I didn't feel any shivering. I slid my hand further up, pausing over her ribs, her withers, and finally under her mane, high up on her neck. No shivering anywhere. She wasn't cold any longer; the quilt was working. And the antibiotics must have kicked in so her temperature had fallen.

I put fresh hay down for both of them and got the wheelbarrow and muck rake to start cleaning up the manure. Right away, the foal spooked at the wheelbarrow and pranced in tight little circles around her mother, snorting at it every time she looked at it. But her stride got longer and slower, and it was obvious she wanted to meet the bright blue creature with the three short legs and no head.

Her circles took her closer and closer to the wheelbarrow and finally she approached it directly, three steps forward, one step back, until she was close enough to stretch her neck out and smell the rim. When it didn't bite or hit or kick, she became braver and stepped close enough to smell all around the rim and then to sniff each wooden handle and then the little tire in front. When she had smelled the whole thing, she tested the rim with her teeth giving it little practice nips all around the edge. When it still didn't nip back, she picked it up with her teeth and flung it as far as she could. It didn't go far, three or four feet but the foal seemed pleased with this. It was the first time I'd seen her ears pricked straight up and her slender legs so still, as she paused to admire her accomplishment. And who could blame her for gloating? She had just killed her first wheelbarrow.

[5]

I T WAS THE middle of April. I'd had Lay Me Down and her foal for three weeks. Rib and hip bones were disappearing under a layer of new fat and muscle. Lay Me Down had lost the bony hump at the base of her mane, her eyes were clear, the wheezing was almost gone.

The Marimekko quilt was gone, too, and in its place she sported a blue New Zealand rug with a polar fleece sweater underneath. I loved her in this getup because I imagined it was a novel experience for her to be both warm and dry. Allie would say I was anthropomorphizing, but I thought the mare was grateful. In fact, I thought most rescued animals exhibited signs of gratitude, an awareness of having been saved from suffering or death, and their gratitude was expressed in a particularly open affection.

Lay Me Down expressed affection by sighing. I saw it as an expression of relief, a letting go of all the tension she'd carried in that big body for such a long time, the horse equivalent of "Phew, I made it."

She sighed a lot. She sighed when I poured the bran mash into her feed bin. She sighed when I put her blankets on at night, and she sighed in the morning when I took them off. She sighed at her hay, she sighed when I brushed her, she sighed when I kissed the end of her nose. She sighed at the vet: great big sighs, big enough to spray me with snot sometimes; loud, wet, affectionate sighs. I loved her sighs. Sometimes I sighed back. I couldn't help it. I wanted her to know I felt the same way. I was relieved, too. "Phew, we've made it," I sighed. We were both safe.

They say you can't escape your past, but I don't believe that. I believe you escape it every day, over and over again, always cognizant of the difference between past and present. Being allowed to live in my own house without being hit, threatened, or ejected would forever remain a novel experience for me. I couldn't imagine taking peace and security for granted. Every morning when I woke up, I luxuriated in the miracle that there was no one in the house who was going to hurt me. I wouldn't walk downstairs for breakfast and be locked in the basement because I'd forgotten to take my clothes out of the dryer the previous day. I wouldn't be told to pack my suitcase and get out. I wouldn't be hit. I'd felt safe for fifteen years, since ending my marriage and buying and moving into this house. I also felt safe since breaking ties with the relatives who had raised me. I luxuriated in the silence in my house, in all the voices that were absent.

Lay Me Down and I were safe, but it turned out the foal wasn't. The case went to court and the owner won.

"You can keep the mare but the foal has to be returned," said a woman on the phone, calling from the SPCA.

I thought I had heard her wrong.

"I'm sorry," she said. "We did everything we could."

I asked her for the name of the judge who had made the decision and then we hung up. It made no sense. Dozens of people had spent thousands of dollars to right a terrible wrong and the court said, "Give them back"? A few minutes later I called the SPCA back and when no one answered, I left a message, protesting the decision. Then I called Allie.

"We can steal her," she said. "We'll keep her in my barn."

I called my lawyer, he had horses, too. He understood this side of me. Still, he advised me against stealing. I hung up, wondering if I had the right lawyer.

The moment I decided to steal the foal, the phone rang. This time it was the director of the SPCA. She explained the court decision in full. Technically, the owner was getting the foals back, but he would have to turn them over to his vet as payment toward his vet bill, which dated from years ago, when the owner still bothered with a vet. The director told me that the owner was required to round up all the foals at their various foster locations and deliver them to his vet.

"He'll be coming *here?*"

"Sometime this afternoon," she replied.

It was the first incomprehensible thing the SPCA had done in this whole case. Giving out the names and addresses of all the foster homes to the former owner of the horses seemed completely irresponsible to me. What was to prevent him from stealing back the mares, from threatening us, from sending one of his cronies over to beat us up, or from chopping off Georgia's head and sticking it under my blanket while I slept?

Allie said she'd come and wait with me so he wouldn't think I lived alone.

"There's strength in numbers," she said.

Oh yeah, I thought, two middle-aged women will really scare this guy. I promised myself I wouldn't open my mouth when he appeared. Not a word. I didn't want to anger him, give him an excuse for being any more of a monster than he already was. Anyway, it was the way I usually dealt with conflict: be silent, smile to death, look at the floor, flee. I did better expressing my anger at the appliances.

I felt ill every time I thought of separating Lay Me Down from her foal. It was too soon and too sudden; the foal wasn't even weaned. I knew people weaned foals as early as six weeks, but I thought it was cruel. I hadn't weaned Sweet Revenge until she was past six months. By then she trusted me, she trusted her environment, and she was completely established on solid food. Also, Georgia had shown signs of being bored with nursing. She walked away abruptly in the middle of being nursed or twitched her tail "no" if she saw her foal approaching.

With the foal gone, Lay Me Down would be alone in her pasture, and horses shouldn't be alone. They're herd animals. The herd provides security, protection, and companionship. I believe it is vital to a horse's sense of well-being to always be with other horses, even if it is only one. It meant I'd have to introduce Lay Me Down to my three sooner than I had planned. If the two geldings had been alone, introducing Lay Me Down could have been done in an afternoon. But introducing one mare to another in an established herd would take longer.

Mares could be difficult to blend. Georgia was possessive of me, the two geldings, the pasture, and the barn. What she saw was what she owned. Her behavior toward other mares could be embarrassing. Sometimes if we trotted past pastured mares, Georgia would pause at the fence long enough to scream and strike, kicking out with a powerful front leg.

Introducing Lay Me Down to Georgia would take a couple of weeks. It meant confining one mare to a stall while the other was loose, in alternation so that contact was limited to sniffing over the stall door. How each mare behaved during each stage determined how soon we could move to the next level of contact.

I wasn't sure about Lay Me Down, but I suspected Georgia would need the full two-week sniff phase. The next step would be to let them meet across a fence, then introduce them face to face on lead lines, then turn them out together in the pasture for short periods of time without the geldings present, and finally, allow all four to be together, loose in the pasture at the same time. The process could easily take a month. Even then I didn't imagine the relationship between Georgia and Lay Me Down would ever amount to more than an uneasy truce. Mares just don't like other mares.

After talking to the SPCA, I called around to some of the other people who had fostered horses and found out quite a bit about the man who was coming to reclaim his foal. I was told that he was originally from Queens before he moved upstate, that he knew nothing about horses, had hired migrant labor for minimal care, and had gambled away his track winnings and everything else.

I didn't like horse racing because I thought it exploited horses, but I understood the thrill of racing, of watching horses thunder around the track. It was impossible not to experience their power vicariously. If you stood close enough to the track, you could feel this power in your chest. As a rider, the power became part of you. One minute you were a smallish human looking at the big tree that had fallen across the path, the next you were half a ton of gorgeous red hair flying over it.

The real problem with horse racing was the money. There was a lot of it and anyone could get lucky. A racehorse owner didn't have to go to college or work his way up from the mail room or wait six months for a small raise. All he had to do was make a small down payment on a racehorse. He didn't even have to know which end went into the starting gate first. Like the man coming to reclaim the foal, he didn't have to know very much to end up with a lot of valuable breeding stock.

Allie arrived right after lunch, and she'd brought along her husband. Rick was calm, good at diffusing tension; he worked in management for a large corporation. He wasn't big but he was smart. His presence would insure a sane, left-brain kind of experience; no emotional outbursts.

"I could give him a boarding bill," I said to Rick. "Tell him he can't take the foal until he pays it."

"If he had any money, the foal wouldn't be here," Rick reminded me.

"It's not too late to steal her," Allie said.

"*Alice*," Rick sighed.

This was why we needed him.

Around two o'clock, a Ford truck pulling a blue four-horse trailer turned into my driveway. Someone had money. Everything looked new—the big truck with the double cab and the shiny blue trailer with all the extras. I didn't want to believe that it belonged to the owner, that he'd spent money on a fancy rig but not on food.

"Maybe it's the vet," I said.

The truck crept down my driveway until it was across the front lawn from us, parallel to where Allie, Rick, and I sat on the back deck. The driver's window rolled down, and a man with thick features and dark hair leaned out.

"Where's da horse?"

Da horse?

"I don't think it's the vet," Allie whispered.

"Straight ahead," Rick called and pointed to the back pasture.

The man didn't answer, didn't even nod. The window rolled up, and the truck moved slowly toward the back pasture. Allie, Rick, and I followed on foot. I was on the edge of crazy, mostly because I thought it was too soon to separate mother and foal, but also because I was afraid of how he'd treat the foal, and I was afraid he'd come back to take Lay Me Down, to hurt me, to hurt my horses, to hurt something. In his mind, horses were all about money, and I was the one who was getting to keep some of what was his.

He pulled the trailer as close to the pasture gate as he could, and then he turned off the engine, and for a second, everything was very quiet. Then two men got out, the driver and another man who looked enough like him to be his brother. They were both tall and fat. They were wearing knit shirts, jeans, and shiny black loafers—city shoes. If it had been 1960 and I had been ten years old, we would have called them greasers. They didn't say anything. They didn't even look at us.

One walked around to the back of the trailer and let down the ramp. He came back with a lead line, and I wanted to laugh. Did he think he was going to walk up to the foal, clip the lead to her halter, and walk her into the trailer like a golden retriever?

Allie must have been thinking the same thing. "You won't need that," she said. "The only way you'll get the foal into the trailer is to get the mother in first."

"I'll get Lay Me Down," I said. I didn't trust either of them to touch her. I didn't trust that once they had her in the trailer they'd let her out again. While they were busy trying to deal with the foal once she was in the trailer, I'd make sure Lay Me Down got out.

It went quickly. Lay Me Down let me lead her into the trailer, and the foal went right in after her. As soon as the foal was inside, I started backing out Lay Me Down. When she saw her mother leaving, the foal squealed, but both men held her, and we made it down the ramp, while Rick closed the back door of the trailer before the foal could escape.

Lay Me Down gave several rapid-fire nickers, showing moderate distress at being separated from her foal. But, as a broodmare, she'd been through this so many times before. For the foal, it was a different story. Lay Me Down stood next to me with her ears forward, listening with the rest of us to the ruckus coming from inside the trailer. It sounded like a soccer game: two teams and everyone playing hard. I wondered how strong the side walls of the trailer were. I wondered if anyone was bleeding. In a few minutes, the driver emerged from the door at the front of the trailer. I was surprised that he still had his front teeth.

"Man," he said, shaking his head.

It was the first thing he'd said since "Where's da horse?" He lit a cigarette and took one deep drag, then flicked the mostly unsmoked cigarette into the long grass.

Whatever had been holding me together didn't last. I could almost hear the snap inside my head—a *ping*, like the sound of a toaster oven when the toast was done—and all of a sudden my dead grandmother showed up, an individual who, during her lifetime, was widely known for possessing no diplomatic skills whatsoever.

"LITTERBUG!" she screamed at him. "Pick up that cigarette!"

Lay Me Down pulled away slightly and looked at me, which is more than I got from the litterbug, who left the cigarette smoldering in the grass and headed for the cab of the truck.

"Um," Rick said, separating himself from me. "Need any help backing out?"

"I hope she kicked the shit out of you!" the reincarnation of Granny called out. But my granny would never have said "shit." It's possible she didn't know the word existed.

"Just keep it real straight through that narrow opening in the stone wall and you should be OK," Rick said as the man swung into the seat and slammed the door in Rick's face. The truck started and began slowly backing down the dirt drive, trailer first.

Allie came over and put her arm around me. "Don't worry," she said, "she definitely kicked the shit out of him."

I felt awful—awful for the foal, awful because I had turned into my grandmother, and awful because Lay Me Down was going to be alone in her pasture that night.

The truck made it to the end of the driveway without hitting anything and backed slowly into the road. Rick and Allie and I stood around Lay Me Down, watching the blue trailer until it disappeared over the crest of a small rise.

We were left with a huge stillness, like an empty school yard after the children have gone home. The air was sweet with pink apple blossoms, blooming in the old orchard behind Lay Me Down's turnout. The pasture grasses had turned a tender green. A pair of killdeer exchanged high-pitched cries as they scuttled around the pasture on long ternlike legs. They would lay their mottled eggs in the middle of the field, perfectly camouflaged on a lichen-covered rock. By mid-July the fledglings would teeter on the fence not too far from the young swallows, all of them taking shaky practice flights across the field. The day the babies flew away for good would feel a lot like this day. Empty. Quiet. Lonely.

"Come for dinner later," Allie called as she and Rick pulled out of my driveway.

After they left, I decided to brush Lay Me Down to help distract her from the foal's absence. She followed me across the pasture into the turnout and waited patiently while I fetched the grooming kit, a long wooden box with a wooden dowel grip filled with combs and brushes. I put it on the ground next to me and pulled out a shed blade: a two-handled flexible aluminum blade with small dull teeth on one side, used to pull out the hair of a horse's thick winter coat.

I started right behind her ears, scraping the blade along her neck in the same direction the hair grew, pulling out the short, dull undercoat as I went. The hair fell to the ground in perfect crescent-shaped clumps. Later, I'd gather up the hair and sprinkle it in the bushes around the pasture for birds to use as nesting material. I had a collection of bird nests in the house, blown down in windstorms, all made with hair from my horses. The nests were incredible works of engineering, some made entirely of horse hair, others mixed with twigs and long grasses.

Lay Me Down pushed her neck against the blade, savoring the feel of a good scratch. Shedding is an itchy business, and most horses enjoy the help of a shedding blade. I had put down some hay to keep her busy while I brushed, but she didn't seem interested in it. Maybe the newly green pasture had spoiled her taste for hay or maybe she just liked being brushed. She looked sleepy. Her head hung low at the end of her long neck, and her eyes gave a slow, droopy blink.

I'd never known a horse this obliging, this relaxed. I was used to being bossed around by Georgia, always on my guard lest I offend her in some way. It didn't seem horsey, this calm, endless good nature. It didn't even seem human. She had so many good reasons to be skittish or mean or difficult, but she never was. Except for when I led her into the trailer, I didn't even keep a halter on her. There was no reason to, she came as soon as she saw me.

Unlike me, Lay Me Down seemed to feel no rancor. In

spite of everything, she was open and trusting of people, qualities I decidedly lacked. It was her capacity to engage that drew me to her, that made me aware of what was possible for me if I had her capacity to...to what? Forgive? Forget? Live in the moment? What exactly was it that enabled an abused animal, for lack of a better word, to love again?

I switched to the other side of her neck and worked backward toward her newly fleshed-out shoulder. She was a pure bay without a single white marking. It made her seem bigger to me, an ocean of deep brown as far as the eye could see.

"You're beautiful," I told her, letting the blade drop and running my hands over the newly sleeked neck. "My Lay Me Downie Brownie," I said.

She took a deep breath and let a fine mist flubber out of her nostrils and slightly parted lips. I felt it on the back of my neck, her big, wet sigh. I felt it on my heart.

[6]

LLIE AND I referred to our young womanhood as colorful. We had been colorful in a lot of the same ways but not together because we hadn't known each other then. We didn't meet until our midthirties, and by then we were in our spiritual phase, grateful we had survived our previous phase. It was the mideighties when we met and lying in the backseat of either one of our cars might have been books like *The Road Less Traveled, Men Who Hate Women,* or the *AA Big Book*.

For some of us, it was news to find out the whole world didn't wake up most mornings hungover, with a man they'd met the night before asleep on the pillow next to them. But that more or less described my twenties if you threw in two packs of Marlboros a day. Somehow I'd managed to get through graduate school and to become a high-school English teacher in Boston.

What I remembered about teaching was the clock, the big round clock at the back of the class, and how long it took the hands to get to noon, when I could leave and eat aspirin for lunch. Afternoon classes were better. The aspirin would start to kick in, and before I knew it, I'd be heading with a group of teachers to Happy Hour at a sports bar in Beacon Circle.

Nobody was happier at Happy Hour than I. By my third glass of white wine the hangover was gone, the shyness was gone, and I was brilliant.

I was pretty and guys liked me. It didn't hurt that I was as hard to pick up as a beer nut. I drank and laughed, gave expert advice on subjects I knew nothing about, danced in my underwear, and hoped everyone noticed how smart I was.

What I really wanted was to buy a horse and get a lot of new riding clothes and be Meryl Streep in *Out of Africa*. First I needed to find a husband, and when I was twenty-nine years old I did. Instead of a baron, my husband was an angry Vietnam vet who looked good in a T-shirt splitting wood. He had once been a world-ranked tennis player and later became the tennis pro at a nearby country club. When he wasn't being surly, he was charming, so we got married and bought a hundred-acre farm in the Africa of America—Vermont.

During the day Jerry taught tennis, and I bought expensive appliances with money I had inherited from my mother.

At night we drank and hurled slurred accusations at each other while gourmet dinners burned on the new Viking range.

A month after we were married, he hit me. From that moment on I hated him, even though a psychiatrist tried to persuade me I didn't.

"Why don't you look at Jerry and tell him how you *really* feel," the doctor would prompt, as though the worst thing the man in the chair next to me had ever done was to leave the toilet seat up. So I'd turn and look deep into Jerry's eyes and say, "I hate you."

This went on for months while I worked up the courage to leave. I would have left the day he hit me except I was embarrassed that my marriage had lasted only a month. Then Jerry had a heart attack. He was only thirty-six years old and, as it turned out, we made it to the emergency room in the nick of time. To be honest, I had mixed feelings about that.

On the spot, Jerry swore off red meat, butter, and Camembert. "What about Scotch?" I asked.

So he swore off Scotch, too, and a few weeks later he was home and sober, cooking Pritikin on the Viking, and I felt trapped. How could I leave someone who faced quadruple bypass surgery within the year?

One night at dinner as I started on the second bottle of wine all by myself, he turned to me and said, "I think you have a drinking problem, too."

Then I really hated him. To get out of the house more, I

went shopping for a horse. Someone had actually loaned me a horse, two horses if you counted the companion pony that came with the pretty bay mare. They had come from a young woman who had left the area to go to college and didn't know when she'd be back. The mare was a quarter horse and her name was April. Our farm bordered state land on all sides with miles of wide dirt logging roads, and I'd go on day-long trail rides with April, letting the pony follow us loose.

But I wanted my own horse, not for showing but for riding trails, jumping fallen trees or stone walls or small streams. I wanted an all-terrain vehicle of a horse, a horse with strength and stamina and beauty. I wanted a Morgan.

I'd never bought my own horse, and I decided to take my time looking for one. Horses can live thirty or forty years, and since I planned on keeping him or her forever, it was important to make the right choice. If only I'd put the same care and thoughtfulness into choosing a husband.

I spent almost a year taking short trips all over New England and New Jersey, Pennsylvania and Ohio, looking at every Morgan for sale and also seeing a lot of other horses besides. At the same time, I knew I'd leave my marriage eventually, so while I was shopping for a horse, I was also looking for an area that could become home.

In late fall about a year after Jerry's heart attack, I found myself in upstate New York. It was cold and windy, and all the leaves were gone as I drove up a long dirt driveway on the way to visit a big Morgan horse breeder who had several horses for sale. On either side of the drive were pas-

tures full of Morgans, five or ten to a field, stretching away
as far as the eye could see. Everywhere fences were in
need of repair, barns needed roofing, and the main house
looked like it hadn't seen a new coat of paint in my lifetime.
In the past year I'd seen all kinds of horse farms, from cli-
mate-controlled stables with airportlike security systems
to simple backyard barns where horses and cows shared a
muddy paddock. This farm looked big and broke. But whatever money the owner still had, she must have put it into
the horses because they looked healthy. I drove slowly and
checked: trimmed feet, shiny coats, clear eyes, good muscle tone. They looked terrific, every single one.

I had spoken to the owner on the phone. Sarah Nichol-
son's voice had been farmer tired and unpretentious. She
told me exactly what I needed to know about her horses
and not a word more. I already knew from the *Morgan
Horse Breeder's Guide* that she owned the top-ranked Morgan
stallion in the country.

I stopped the car at one of the enormous falling-down
barns at the end of the drive. It must have been a dairy barn
once; there were a few cow stanchions still visible at one
end. I got out of the car and looked around for a human
being. The barnyard was full of odd bits of farm equipment,
chickens scratching around in the dirt, barn cats sunning in
the doorway, and a couple of scraggly-looking black dogs
who came over and peed on my tires. But no people.

I could see the color of the air that day, clear and sharp,
the way the light is in late fall, the sun low in the west,

bouncing off all those shiny rumps in fields that were still green. In the distance I could hear cars on the New York State Thruway, a steady hum floating on the wind across the wide-open fields. The barnyard smelled of manure, diesel fuel, and hay.

And then, in the distance, perhaps a quarter of a mile away, turning into the same dirt drive I had just driven down, I saw my horse. There's a line I read in a book once: *I knew it was her by the feel of my heart in my chest.* That's how it was for me.

All I could really see from that distance was a chestnut-colored Morgan with a wavy red mane pulling an open two-wheeled cart driven by a large man holding a buggy whip. But the word *pulling* didn't do justice to what the horse was doing to that cart. Maybe it was the excitement of the wind, lifting and twirling her mane like towels on a clothes-line, or maybe it was the sight of the barn, signaling the last stretch toward a bucket of grain, a warm stall, and some sweet hay. She seemed out of control.

She'd look great for fifteen seconds or so, with an extended, high-stepping trot, pretty as any carriage horse in a period film. Then suddenly she'd toss her head and buck, kick the cart behind her, break into a run, jerk the cart from one side of the road to the other, and just as suddenly resume the pretty trot. It was a miracle she didn't run into the fence or overturn the cart. The other miracle was that her driver never once used his whip or raised his voice. I could hear him talking to her, but he didn't yell, even at her most out-of-control moments. By the time they reached me, I wanted to take them both home.

The driver's name was Bob and he was a professional horse trainer. The red horse was a three-year-old named Georgia, who had just completed her first lesson in harness.

"What a brat," I said, holding the reins near her perfect head as Bob stepped down from the cart. I had to stand right in front of her in order to see her whole face around the blinders. She had enormous almond-shaped eyes and a small white star in the middle of her forehead. Her Arabian ancestry was visible in the pronounced cheekbones and narrow, slightly scooped nose. Her chest and withers were covered in foamy white sweat, and she smelled like wet leather.

Bob looked like a farmer from Lake Woebegon, a character right out of the Garrison Keillor radio show. He had to be six and a half feet tall, and there was no other way to put it: he was fat. He wore baggy jean coveralls that didn't quite make it to his ankles and a plaid flannel shirt with the cuffs rolled back, exposing long underwear with a lot of holes. He had smooth white skin with a pinkish tint and long, thick fingers.

"She's got a way to go," he smiled, laying a pink hand on Georgia's rump and leaving it there.

I liked the way he touched her, the way he left his hand on her back quietly like that. No slapping, even affectionately, nothing that would startle her. She chewed her bit and shifted her weight from foot to foot, pushing me away with her nose. She kept turning her head to look for Bob, for anything, trying to see around her blinders. She was a busy horse, and if we'd just get out of the way, she'd be down the road and halfway to Lake Wobegon by breakfast.

At some point Sarah showed up. She was skinny, in her midfifties, chain-smoking Chesterfields. Her limp brown hair was held in a ponytail with the kind of elastic they put around the broccoli at the grocery store. It looked like she'd been pulling all-nighters her whole life; there was enough skin under her eyes to make a burrito. The teeth she had were OK; it was the ones that were missing you noticed, mainly on the sides, which explained the supermodel cheeks. She had on jeans, old blue sneakers, and a gray sweatshirt that zipped up the front with a hood. Underneath that sweatshirt was another sweatshirt without a hood. She wasn't much of a talker.

"This one's not for sale," she said, flicking the ash of her cigarette toward Georgia. She started walking off, I supposed in the direction of the horses who *were* for sale.

I didn't budge. When she realized I wasn't behind her, she stopped and turned around.

"If she *was* for sale, what would she cost?" I asked. I wasn't leaving until I had a piece of paper in my hand saying I owned this horse. I'd looked at so many Morgans—some prettier, some bigger, all of them better behaved—but only this one had leapt into my heart.

"She's a mess, that one," Sarah said, shaking her head. But she wasn't shaking her head as in no, you can't have her ever, ever, ever. It was more like, why would you *want* to?

"Yeah, I saw," I said. I was pretty sure I could fix that mess. Anyway, I didn't want to drive her, I wanted to ride her.

Sarah lit a fresh cigarette off the stub of the one recently clamped between her lips and thought for a second. Bob had slipped the wooden shafts out of the harness and was backing the carriage toward the side of the barn. I was still standing near Georgia's head, holding the reins, wishing she'd show a little more interest in me and a little less in the dead weeds she couldn't reach because I wouldn't let her. She was still wet from the driving lesson and needed to be walked until she was dry. Most big farms had an electric horse walker, a contraption that looked like a large circular clothesline to which you could hook four horses, to be walked in a slow circle until they were dry. If Sarah had one, it was nowhere in sight.

"She's green broke English and western," Sarah told me. "We had her down at the Garden last spring in Western Pleasure, just to give her some practice. I got a nice proof you could have made up."

The Garden meant a show at Madison Square Garden, and in a Western Pleasure event the rider uses a western saddle and puts the horse through a series of walks, trots, and canters, as though riding for pleasure. A proof was a photograph. But what she was really saying was that she'd be willing to sell this horse.

"I ride English," I said. In my head I was jumping up and down shouting, *She's mine! She's mine!*

"Could be a good endurance horse," Sarah said. "She has

plenty of heart, good strong legs and feet, and loves to eat."

"I do a lot of trail riding," I told her. Our conversation was getting positively chummy: two moms discussing the future of a kid we both knew wasn't going to Harvard.

"Of course, she'll do better as she matures, when she's five or six," Sarah said. "If you want, Bob could work with her some more before you take her."

She was mine, just like that. But for how much? Sarah still hadn't said. I had budgeted ten thousand dollars to spend on a horse. Not a lot by horse standards, but I wasn't buying a horse for showing, I was buying a horse for pleasure riding. Even with her breeding, sired by the number-one-standing Morgan stallion, I didn't think Georgia would cost anywhere near ten thousand.

"Can I walk her out?" I asked, suddenly anxious about keeping a wet horse standing still on a cold day. *My* wet horse. It would also give me a chance to be alone with her to see how she moved and behaved off the bit, to see if she'd listen to me.

Sarah threw her cigarette in the dirt and walked toward the barn. "I'll get a halter and lead."

Georgia and I followed her into the barn, and I helped Bob take off her harness. Then Bob towel-dried her and brushed her down. It only took a few minutes and when she was ready, I clipped a lead line to the chin ring of her leather halter and led her out to the long dirt drive.

It was about five o'clock, and the sun had disappeared behind a forest of evergreens on the horizon. The light was fading, and the air smelled of wood-burning stoves and horses. The hum of cars on the thruway was steady in the distance, punctuated by the muted roar of trucks and tractor trailers. The wind had died down, but it was still breezy enough for Georgia's mane to flicker across my face as we walked down the drive past fields of Morgans.

I walked, Georgia trotted. We passed dozens of grazing horses on either side of the dirt drive, and Georgia was very much aware of them. Her head swiveled from one side of the road to the other with wide nostrils, keeping up a low, throaty nicker.

Her high-stepping trot was due in part to the shoes she was wearing. They were called trailers, a heavy shoe, designed to make a horse throw the foot high, creating that prancing effect often seen in carriage horses and saddlebreds. As lovely as it looked, to me it seemed contrived and unnatural. I'd get Georgia's removed and replaced with plain shoes as soon as I could.

She was three years old, and I was thirty. With any luck, we'd be together until I was in my sixties. That was a commitment, a word I hated. I thought it meant the opposite of freedom. I thought it meant you were trapped, stuck, buried. Life was over and now you had this obligation, this ever-present other who said things like "And where were you?" and "How much did it cost?" and "Why didn't you call?"—all the none-of-your-business questions that were suddenly OK because you had a commitment. Some people called it love. I called it a burden.

I was thinking this because I wanted Georgia to pay attention to me and she wasn't. I wanted her to be as enthralled with me as I was with her, to feel that same chest-tugging connection. Instead, she was thinking about ditching the stranger tugging at her pretty head so she could run off and frisk with the other three-year-olds. She wasn't interested in a doting new mommy, she was interested in grazing.

I wish I could say all that insight saved my marriage, that I ran home to Jerry and the new Sub-Zero filled with organic mesclun and free-range eggs to say how sorry I was for being unforgiving and unavailable; for being a lush and a cheap lush, too—Gallo, $4.95 a gallon. Maybe Jerry was no prize but neither was I.

I think it was the idea of being with Georgia for the next thirty years that made me think about my life and where it was going, like deciding to have a child and realizing it meant having to change some things first. I didn't want to bring anyone into the lie that was my life, not even a horse.

At the very least, it meant taking the steps to end my marriage. Forget about saving face or saving Jerry, it was time to save myself.

We walked until Georgia was dry and it was getting too dark to see where we were going. She never settled down, dancing and bucking at the end of the lead, but it didn't change how I felt about her or how eager I was to get those awful shoes off her.

I took her back and put her in one of the big box stalls

in the dairy barn that had only partially been converted for horses. Then Sarah and I hung over the stall door for a while and watched her eat grain. She had a blue-ribbon face with a low tail set and a beautifully arched but short neck. These flaws would eliminate her from being shown in a halter class or being considered good breeding stock. Still, she was classic Morgan with the deep chest, the rounded neck, and the chiseled Arab face. Her coloring wasn't a flaw, but red (called chestnut) was not popular with Morgan enthusiasts. In show circles it was well known that judges were prejudiced against chestnut Morgans. I had always wanted a chestnut, though, and, looking at her, it was impossible to imagine why everyone didn't feel the same.

We were quiet a long time, and then Sarah spoke. "Three thousand and you pay for shipping," she said.

Three thousand seemed too low. Surely it would be shortchanging Sarah. "Who'd do the shipping?" I asked.

"Me," she said.

"When?"

"Whenever you want."

"Tomorrow?"

"Just gimme the directions."

Oh my. Thirty years.

[7]

I WENT HOME, and the next day Georgia arrived, and then it was time to tell my husband I was leaving, but I didn't. I was waiting for the right moment. Whatever that moment would look like, I didn't know, but I waited for it anyway.

While I waited I schooled Georgia on a lunge line, which is a long rope with a person at one end and a horse on the other. The horse moves in circles around the person, practicing walk, trot, and canter by voice command. When we both had had enough of that, I saddled her up and rode her over miles of logging roads through fragrant white pines. At night I drank Gallo.

I did some terrible things when I was drunk. I drove a hundred and ten miles an hour in my new Saab and never gave a second thought to the cars I flew past, or if I did, it was only to feel superior. Once I drove to Boston to catch a plane for Aspen. I left the house late because I was too hungover to get up, and an hour before my flight was due to take off, I still had a hundred miles to go. I got a ticket for driving a hundred miles per hour: driving to endanger. I remember the officer's eyes as I waved my airline ticket at him in a fury, blaming him because I would miss my flight. His eyes were big and unblinking, and I saw in them a mix of shock and pity as he listened to the screaming bitch on the side of the highway.

I'd owned Georgia for six months, and she was turning into a dream horse. I rode her all winter, through deep snow on which she seemed to float and even at night, if there was enough moon to light the way. On bitter cold days I rode her bareback to keep me warm. I rode her to get through hangovers and to get away from the ongoing arguments with my husband. I rode her because it was the only thing left in my life I wasn't doing wrong.

One night in March, my husband started drinking again, and I knew it was the right moment to leave. The truth was, the right moment to leave had come and gone a long time before the night the bottle of Scotch reappeared, so it was too late to pack or plan or do anything but grab a coat and run for the Saab.

I drove all the way to Boston, four hours straight, right to the house of my friend Barbara, a teacher from the group that used to go to Happy Hour together. Barbara drank extra-dry martinis and had great legs. Not that she was ugly, but it was her legs people remembered. She used to say it took a lot of gin to fill up those legs.

Even though I arrived unexpectedly in the middle of the night, we sat at her kitchen counter—Barbara drinking martinis, me drinking white wine—and talked about what a drunken lout my husband was, and no wonder I'd left him. Someone as wonderful as I was deserved better. Then we talked about all the teachers we knew at school and why their lives were sad and dull, what with husbands and babies and dirty diapers, compared to ours, which were full of interesting moments like, for instance, this talk we were having in the middle of the night in her kitchen.

"We wanago blazes, nodsid aroun withabunge of kirty dids."

"Thazo true."

We woke up late the next day and faced each other, pale and shaky, across the kitchen counter again. This time she said, "What do you say we don't drink today?"

I said all right, never for a moment believing she meant it. *I* certainly didn't, but that's what you say when someone casually mentions not drinking. Then she suggested we get the Sunday paper.

She parked in front of a drugstore and went in to get the paper while I sat in the passenger seat with the sun visor pulled down, shading my eyes behind sunglasses even though it was overcast and almost dark enough to be dusk. I looked at my watch. *It was dusk.* It was six o'clock. We'd slept all day.

When she came back, she sat in the driver's seat, riffling through the paper, throwing most of it into the backseat and studying a single page in her lap before she finally looked up and said, "Want to go to church?"

"Church?" Maybe I had heard her wrong.

"Not exactly church," she said. "There's an AA meeting in the basement of a church right around the corner."

My face hurt everywhere my sunglasses touched, and if I moved too fast, the whole world spun so I was careful not to overreact and whip my head around to stare at Barbara. But I was dumbfounded. She might as well have said, *Want to go knock over a mini-mart?* AA? It was too awful, too humiliating.

Barbara started to cry. "I'm tired of feeling like this," she said, sniffling into a Kleenex. "Do what you want, but I'm going."

I felt like a terrible friend because she had asked me to do something, and I hadn't said yes, and now she was crying. Last night she'd thrown the front door open and hugged me even though it was midnight and she didn't know I was coming, and now all she wanted was for me to go someplace with her for an hour. It was the least I could do. Besides, maybe if she went to an AA meeting, she'd realize she should stop drinking gin and switch to drinking wine like me. Then we could just forget about this little episode.

"Think any interesting men will be there?" I said.

Later I wouldn't remember the meeting or whether there had been interesting men. I also didn't remember calling my husband to tell him I wasn't coming back, but the real surprise was that I stopped drinking. Not just because of AA, but because after one night of not drinking, I wanted to see if I could stop for two nights, then three, and so on. It was a game, like learning to hold your breath underwater, something uncomfortable but rewarding. Suddenly you're swimming the whole length of the pool without coming up for air, and you think it's amazing until you break your own record and swim two lengths. Then you're hooked. All you want to know after that is, *How far can I go with this?*

However, it only felt like a game for the first few weeks. After that, it felt like coming out of a coma and realizing all the ways I'd been left behind during the ten years I'd been in a vegetative state. The void in my life created by not drinking was larger than anything I'd ever experienced. If I didn't drink, what was the point? What did I *do?*

I missed drinking but I didn't miss the hangovers. For the first time in my adult life I had mornings, a whole chunk of day I'd never known about before. I'd perceived them hazily, when I could perceive them at all, as something to survive, something to get through. Now I really had them. I could get up and eat breakfast. I could ride Georgia first thing, before the bugs got bad. I could canter around in the woods near the new house I had bought after I left Jerry.

It was a miracle, having mornings. I couldn't get over how beautiful they were. It was like being at summer camp again with a feeling of excitement each dawn because the day ahead was going to be full of horses and sweet-smelling air. And no one was going to hit me because I finally lived alone. It was the first house that was all mine, where no one could tell me to get out or make me feel unwelcome. I had bought it a month after I stopped drinking. So mornings were good. They were really, really good.

Nights, on the other hand, were awful. Dinner parties were something to survive, especially if liquor was served. Blind dates (or any situation that smacked of a fix-up by well-meaning new friends) were out of the question. Without liquor I couldn't function socially. I couldn't make small talk or flirt or laugh. I felt like a child trapped at the grown-ups' table. Conversation around me sparkled with talk about terrific jobs, fabulous children, trips abroad. I was the retired Gallo expert who stared in amazement at the wineglasses people left half empty when they got up to leave the table. *Hey,* I wanted to say, *how can you leave that?* I got quieter and quieter and eventually I stopped going to parties at all. I spent my days and nights alone.

With all that peace and quiet I had plenty of time to think, and what I thought about was beginning that novel I'd been wanting to write ever since I was seven. It was the other thing I loved besides horses: books. I loved reading them, and I couldn't imagine anything better than growing up and writing one. When I became a teacher, it was always in the back of my mind to use summers and school vacations as a time to write. I wrote poetry, kept a journal, and briefly freelanced as a feature writer for a small Boston paper, but in spite of all this, I'd never gotten serious about writing.

I needed to support myself, and the chances of making a living as a novelist were slim. After burning through my inheritance on expensive appliances (no longer mine), a house, and a horse, I needed a job. I had liked teaching but I always found myself wondering why smart students failed or why some students hated school or smoked at twelve or rebelled in other ways. I wondered about the other teachers, too: why they said what they said and did what they did. I wondered about people all the time, mostly about the unhappy ones. There seemed to be so many, including me. Mornings were lucid, and my days were peaceful and calm, but I couldn't say I ever felt happy. I felt grateful sometimes, not happy. There was a difference. I was relieved but not energized.

Therefore, while working in the office of a local alcohol treatment center, I returned to night school for a master's degree in social work. By my midthirties, I was counseling in a residential drug-treatment program during the day and teaching social work classes at the local community college at night.

I felt as turned around as Eliza Dolittle. There seemed to be no connection between my former life and my new life, except for horses. Horses were the thread that had been there from the beginning, through the pain of childhood and the drinking and the marriage, the thread that seemed to keep me stitched together. Georgia was, in a sense, my therapist. For years she listened to my rantings as we tore around the woods. I couldn't help it. I needed an ear and there they were, two big ones, right in front of me. Georgia needed someone, too, so less than a week after she was returned to me in the divorce settlement, I acquired Hotshot to keep her company and, a few weeks later, Tempo. And eleven months later, there was the surprise arrival of Georgia's foal, Sweet Revenge.

Despite the business of the new career, the new house, the new life, the urge to write a book did not subside with the passage of time. I'd been saying I wanted to write for twenty years. I'd said it so often and for so long that people who knew me didn't even hear it anymore. It was just one of those things I repeated, like "I should re-gravel the driveway."

"I want to write a book," I said to Allie.

"Did I tell you about that eagle?"

"I just can't think of anything to write." I'd throw up my hands.

"I was in my kayak and this eagle was standing there, not twenty feet away, playing with a snorkeling mask somebody must have left on the beach last summer."

"*Other* people write books, why can't I?"

"A bald eagle!"

"Wow," I said, "a bald eagle."

Even though I said it all the time and no one listened anymore when I did, the secret was, I meant it. I'd always meant it. Actually, the real secret was stranger than wanting to write a book. The real secret was that I already thought of myself as a writer. I'd hardly written a word and I couldn't think of a single idea for a book, but in my mind, I was a writer. I'd been a writer since I was seven.

Thirty-five years is a long time to carry around an idea about yourself that has no foundation in reality; it was as if I secretly thought I was the Grand Duchess Anastasia. The evidence was so slim that a pessimist might say it was non-existent. But I was pregnant with book. I could feel it kicking to get out. I was one of those women designed by nature to write books: wide in the hips, perfect for long hours sitting at the computer. I could birth a lot of books with those hips, if I could just get started.

Yet I didn't get started. For the next two months my days were full. Mornings before work I rode Georgia. All day I counseled clients, taught at the college, and once home again, I nursed Lay Me Down back to health. I worried about my bad back and the gray hairs appearing on my head faster than I could pluck them out. I had always promised myself I wouldn't be one of those women who clung to youth when youth was gone. No collagen, no surgery, no expensive creams that promised to reduce or eliminate wrinkles. When the time came, I'd throw out the short skirts, the clingy tops, anything with Lycra, and just look and dress my age. But accepting age was harder than I'd expected. More than the physical changes and the chucking of the accoutrements of youth, the hardest part of middle age was realizing that time was finite. The more gray hair I saw in the mirror, the worse I felt about not writing. I was like a woman facing forty who was desperate for a baby.

A few weeks after her foal left, it was time to blend Lay Me Down into the herd. She'd gained a hundred pounds since I'd gotten her (you weighed horses with a measuring tape that gave pounds instead of feet and inches), her lungs were clear, and she was lonely. She grazed near the gate of her pasture even though there was better grass farther away. If she stayed near the gate she could see the other three horses, and my sense was that just seeing them helped her feel like part of the herd.

I didn't introduce her to both geldings at once, as planned. My instinct now told me to bring Hotshot to Lay Me Down's pasture and leave them alone to get acquainted. Hotshot was old and sweet, Lay Me Down was crippled from racing and lonely, and there wasn't a mean bone in either of their bodies. What could happen?

Georgia and Tempo made a big fuss as I led Hotshot out of the pasture and shut the gate, leaving them behind. They both kept up a frantic whinnying, rushing back and forth along the fence as though terrified.

Not Hotshot. He was definitely the gentleman caller on his way to sit on the front porch with someone special. He'd been looking at Lay Me Down for a month, and it was like this was the dating game, and he'd won. He was ready. He'd lost most of his winter coat, and he looked sleek and shiny. He was almost a perfect match in color to Georgia's red.

People who saw them for the first time had a hard time telling them apart.

In the order of dominance—there is always a clear and rigid pecking order with horses—Hotshot was at the bottom. In some herds, establishing the pecking order could be a rough business involving loud, physical confrontations. That had never happened with my three. Within minutes of being together for the first time, they had worked out that Tempo was the wise and gentle ruler, Georgia was the bitchin' babe who got away with obnoxious behavior just because, and Hotshot was the good-natured nanny who doted on the other two, even when he was Georgia's punching bag. This had been worked out nonverbally and nonviolently as they stood in a tight circle, all three noses together in the middle. Every once in a while a head had jerked up, but in a few seconds the noses were together again. This went on for five or so minutes, and then they started grazing, and that was that.

Hotshot was all arched neck and big eyes as we headed over to Lay Me Down's pasture. His eagerness to meet her was touching given his experience with females. He'd taken so much abuse from Georgia in the past ten years. Who was to say this one wouldn't be the same? But that didn't seem to be what he was thinking as he tugged at the lead, hurrying me along toward Lay Me Down's pasture.

Lay Me Down had seen us coming and stood with her chest pressed against the gate, waiting. Her head was high, her ears up and forward as she blew out a little whinny.

Hotshot whinnied back. They were talking. I was dying to know what they were saying. *Hello? You can come over but don't pull any funny stuff? After all these weeks I can't believe we're finally meeting? This place has great grass, don't you agree?*

We arrived at the gate and right away they touched noses for a good long sniff. This was one of the prettiest yet most tension-fraught moments of introducing two horses. The outcome of a face-to-face meeting was impossible to predict and might or might not involve some form of physical aggression. With Georgia, a meeting with any new horse, particularly another mare, almost certainly involved violence. When a horse in the wild wants to attack something, it uses its front legs to do so. The kick can be devastating, even lethal.

I was relieved but not surprised when neither Hotshot nor Lay Me Down exhibited any kind of aggression whatsoever. They sniffed and whinnied softly at each other, and after a few minutes I pushed gently at Lay Me Down's chest to move her away from the gate so I could open it. She backed up just enough for Hotshot to squeeze through, I unclipped the lead line, and he trotted right in.

I stood at the gate and watched two sweet old horses go a-courting. Their mutual attraction was instant and strong, and to a human eye—say that of a lonely middle-aged person with a tendency toward anthropomorphizing—it looked romantic. Hotshot's nose spent a lot of time moving from one end of Lay Me Down's long neck to the other, and when he felt braver, he let it wander past her shoulder right to the middle of her back. She grazed. He sniffed. She grazed some more, he sniffed. She moved, he moved and sniffed. She wandered over to the watering trough for a drink, he wandered over and sniffed. He couldn't believe she was for real. She was nothing like Georgia. She was nice.

She liked him, too. She seemed to understand that the sniffing wasn't going anywhere heavy, so she'd put up with it until the infatuation ran its course and they could move on to being a herd—a herd of two, but a herd. She knew this first. Deep down he knew, too, but sometimes he forgot he was gelded. Georgia had no trouble reminding him he was useless for that sort of thing with a quick incisor to the neck, but Lay Me Down let him dream for a while. She looked at me and sighed. *Can he stay?* she seemed to ask.

Hours later I looked out the window, and Lay Me Down was grazing with Hotshot standing at a right angle to her shoulder, no longer sniffing but still not composed enough to think about grass. She was much taller than he was; he had to lift his head to look over her back. Her legs were long and slender compared to his shorter, stockier ones. Her neck, too, was long and slender; his was shorter and thicker. She was every inch a racing machine; he was every inch a dude-ranch dude. Together, they were a duet of contentment. I was happy for both, for Hotshot to have a break from Georgia's relentless bossing and for Lay Me Down to have a companion.

Tempo and Georgia had moved away from the fence and returned to grazing, all signs of distress about Hotshot's departure gone. Occasionally, one or the other looked up, saw Hotshot in the distance, and, satisfied that he was within sight, returned to grazing.

I decided to leave them this way indefinitely, in contented couples. I was pretty sure if I added Tempo to the pasture with Lay Me Down and Hotshot, things would go as smoothly as they had with Hotshot, but that would have meant leaving Georgia alone, and I didn't think she'd tolerate that, not for long. Besides, it would have been unfair to leave her alone while her two boys were in plain sight with another horse.

The next step was bringing the mares together, and I dreaded it. I knew Georgia too well to have any illusions about how she'd behave. Sometimes I wondered what had possessed me to get another horse, or if I had to, why it couldn't have been a gelding. I blamed myself for creating a monster, a monster named Georgia. All these years of spoiling her, of never allowing anyone else to ride her, of letting her boss me around the same way she bossed around Hotshot and Tempo and the vet. I wondered why I had knowingly, willingly, *eagerly* paid money for a discipline problem. From the moment I saw her, I had known she was trouble, yet I couldn't wait to get her home to my barn.

Sometimes I wondered if I would ever love a human being as much as I loved Georgia. This troubled me. And the older I got, the more it troubled me. I didn't want to be one of those people whose obituary mentioned only surviving loved ones with hooves.

What I really wondered was, could I love a man? I loved my women friends. I loved my brother, his wife, and his three children, I loved my neighbors, and I loved Allie. I even loved people I'd never met, like Jane Austen for writing her books, Wolf Kahn for his pastels, and Franz Marc for his paintings of horses.

Yet I didn't love a man. Not that way. I wondered if something was wrong with me, if I was one of those people incapable of intimacy. It would have made sense if I was, but I didn't want to be.

"Why don't men like me?" I asked a social worker friend whose honesty, insight, and frankness I particularly valued.

She paused for two seconds, possibly less. "Because of what they see," she said.

I swallowed hard. *She thought I was ugly*. "What do they see?" But I didn't really want to hear her answer. It was obvious she was pathologically abrasive and couldn't be trusted.

"They see a big wall," she said, "with a sign that reads KEEP OUT."

I was so relieved she didn't say, *Sorry, but men just find you repulsive* that the notion that I was walling myself off seemed acceptable. "Good fences make good neighbors," I said.

"Yeah, but your wall is covered with ice and giant thorn bushes and along the top is razor wire, and the whole thing is electrified, and there are these armed guards with nuclear weapons and..."

"I get the picture. But if I don't know I'm doing that, how do I stop?"

"Thaw and disarm."

I practiced thawing in the grocery store. When I ran into a male shopper, I didn't dive behind my grocery list. I looked into his eyes and smiled, or if I couldn't manage that, I looked at his shoes instead of down at mine. One day I was in the farmer's market near where I lived, picking out a pie.

"Which do *you* think is the best pie?" asked a deep voice right next to me.

His presence caught me so off guard that I had to jerk my head away from the pies I'd been contemplating, and before any entrenched behavior had a chance, I was looking into his smiling brown eyes and smiling right back. He was handsome, too, and tall, dressed country casual, the way I loved a man to dress, as though he wasn't going to let a staggering stock portfolio get in the way of the fact that he just felt more comfortable in stained khakis and Birkenstocks.

"Blueberry," I said, tossing my newly highlighted locks off my forehead. I felt bold and wild, as if underneath my sweats I was wearing a garter belt.

"Blueberry?" he said meaningfully.

"Honey!" a female voice called from the entrance. "The kids are getting spastic in the backseat."

I followed his eyes to Audrey Hepburn, who stood in the doorway in tiny cutoffs and a wedding ring. It was too painful to look at her for more than a long glance. She made me feel like throwing myself on the steps at Lourdes and wailing, *Why these legs?*

"Be right there, hon," his full lips answered, and he swept up a blueberry pie with one fuzzy hand. "Thanks for the tip." He smiled and tore himself away with depressingly little effort.

I told myself this was just the warm-up. Something to remind me to stop wearing pajamas to the store. Let's face it, if you sleep in sweats, technically that makes them pajamas. Men don't like women in pajamas, not even in bed. It all came back to me, how it was to be with a man, how none of them had ever said, "If you're going to wear those sweats, you better be packing birth control."

Sweats were the razor wire of my wardrobe, and they worked. There hadn't been a break-in for ten years. To be honest, I wasn't sure anyone had been interested in trying, unless you counted the men I counseled at work, who woke up off drugs for the first time in twenty years so desperately needy that they were like baby ducks, imprinting on the first thing they saw.

Besides clients, I hardly ever met men. Social work was a woman's world. I knew male social workers existed, but they were as rare as red beach glass. Besides, a man with good communication skills just wasn't my type. No man I'd been with had ever said, "Sweetie, let's just sit down and work this out."

Maybe that was the problem. My type was modeled on my father, and men like my father turned out to be, well, men like my father: bright, funny, rejecting. Or, as his fourth wife put it, "Terrific, until you got to know him." I spent years waiting for my father to notice me. And that was after years spent waiting for him to just show up. I was never more than minimally interesting to my father, and even then, it was mostly as a target for his humor or his wrath. My father was a lot like my first pony, Bunty. Both returned my love with a mean bite.

However, I knew my social worker friend was right. I didn't have to be the impaired rat who kept going back for the shock. I could be the smart rat, the rat who chose pleasure instead of pain, the Christopher Columbus rat, willing to fall off the edge of the earth rather than go the same old route. I was so ready, ready to be that daring, adventurous rat who discovers a whole new world.

If Lay Me Down could risk loving, so could I.

[8]

I SAT ON an upended cinder block, reading the newspaper in the sunny doorway of the barn. It was one of my favorite places to sit, especially in May when the swallows swooped in and out, busy with nesting. That day, however, I sat listening to Georgia pace around her stall, whinnying in fury because Lay Me Down was out in the pasture. It was Lay Me Down's turn to be outside with the boys, while Georgia remained in her stall. I'd been rotating them, one in, one out, for three days. Georgia was behaving as I'd imagined she would. When I let the mares sniff noses over the stall door, Georgia squealed and struck the door. Lay Me Down looked alarmed and backed away.

The meeting between Lay Me Down and Tempo had gone smoothly. The only glitch had been Hotshot's proprietary behavior toward Lay Me Down, which created minor tension between the geldings for the first time in the thirteen years they'd been together. Hotshot was never farther than a few feet from Lay Me Down and always positioned between her and Tempo. If Tempo got too close, Hotshot flattened his ears and rushed at him, warning him away. Tempo accepted the warning and moved off without objection.

Lay Me Down seemed irritated by the intensity of Hotshot's attachment. I know I would have been. He shadowed her everywhere and wouldn't let her get close to Tempo even when she initiated it. He hovered by her stall door when it was her turn to be confined. Sometimes she flattened her ears and flicked her tail at him but that was as angry as she ever got. It was good to see she could assert herself even though it made no difference. Hotshot didn't budge from her side.

I sat in the sunny doorway, within sight of Georgia so she wouldn't be alone, hoping my presence would help soothe her agitation. It did a little. There were longer stretches of quiet between the pacing and whinnying, when I knew she was either eating hay or resting from the exhaustion of being angry for three days.

She'd been quiet so long I'd been able to read the whole paper, including the classifieds. I wasn't selling or buying anything, I didn't need a job, and even though I was a daring Christopher Columbus rat now, I'd rather have been single forever than answer an ad in the personals.

Then something stranger than answering a personal ad happened. I went in for lunch and the phone rang.

"Hello, Susan," a male voice said, "this is Hank Dolby. We met six years ago at a party at the Gardners' house."

I was instantly confused. I remembered meeting him, but I couldn't imagine why he was calling except for some horrible reason: mutual friends had been killed in a freak accident, my ex-husband had moved next door and was asking about me in a suspicious way, I had done something awful. My mind was spinning. Nobody just called out of the blue. He and his wife were writers and lived in a small town on the other side of the Hudson River. The wife was tall and opinionated with beautiful skin. Hank was shorter and quieter with thinning red hair and twinkly, observant eyes. Their pretty young daughter had been at the party, too, and when I met them at the Gardners' that night, I remembered thinking they were a family who had it all: brains, beauty, and books.

"I remember you," I said, straining to sound composed.

"How are you doing?" he asked. "Last time we talked you were on your way to England."

Is that why he was calling, to find out how my trip to England had been? Six years later?

"It was sunny the whole time." This felt crazy, telling him about six-year-old weather.

We talked like that for a few more minutes, stuck in the past.

Then suddenly he said, "Are you with anyone?"

I thought he was asking if anyone was in the room with me, as though he was going to tell me a secret, and he wanted to make sure I was alone. Then I understood.

"Not really."

He told me he'd been divorced for a year and felt ready to "get out there again," as he put it. Would I like to have dinner next Saturday?

"I'd love to," I said, but what I really meant was, I'd love to be able to. I'd love to be able to throw on a little black dress and head out the door next Saturday night like thousands of women all over America. That he'd asked, that he'd remembered me six years later and called was enough excitement. The miracle had already happened. Getting to know him could ruin it. But I can't tell him that. I said I'd love to. I could call and cancel later.

Being asked for a date was big news, big enough to make me want to tell someone, so I called my brother, Lloyd, a lawyer who lived in Vermont with his wife and three children. I could count on getting the sensitive male perspective from my brother.

"He's probably going through his Rolodex and it took him a year to get to the Rs," he said.

I could also count on getting the *insensitive* male perspective, the reality check. It was impossible to forget that I was the *God-you're-so-dumb* little sister, still getting my nose flicked every time I fell for the *What's this on the front of your shirt?* routine. That was my earliest memory of him. I trusted him, and he tripped me every chance he got.

After our mother died and our father left, for a few brief weeks we crawled into each other's beds at night and whispered about what was to become of us. On one of those nights he gave me a piece of Juicy Fruit gum, the first thing he had ever given me, and it was as though he had given me the Hope Diamond. Those few weeks huddled together at night, along with the gift of gum, created a connection to him that was so strong in me it survived the next twenty years we were to be separated.

By our forties, our pattern hadn't changed much. Sometimes I got tripped, and sometimes I got Juicy Fruit gum, but our connection was deep and unbreakable. We liked to talk about the past.

When I'd visit him in Vermont we'd sit around the table after dinner and start talking about *What Had Happened*.

"What was it like before she died?" I'd ask. I had almost no memories of our mother, no memories of our family doing anything together. My brother was seven when she died, I had been five. He remembered a lot.

"In the summer we'd go to the beach," he'd say. "Dad liked to cook out on the beach."

"Did we have fun?" I'd ask. "Did Mom and Dad get along?"

"Sometimes," he'd say. "She didn't like his drinking."

After a while, my brother's wife and three teenage children would start to fidget, and one by one, they'd slip away from the table and leave us to our excavating.

"Did she know she was dying?"

He'd nod. "She told me to take care of you."

And in a way he had. Not then, not when he was seven and sent away to a boarding school in South Carolina that had created a third grade especially for him. And not during the years when I was sent from relative to relative and eventually to a boarding school in Massachusetts in eighth grade. It was after college, when we were both in graduate school in Boston, that we started to get together regularly. Two or three times a week I'd drive to his house in the suburbs, and we'd take a walk or have dinner and catch up on the past.

I needed to do that. I needed to know what had happened to us and, as much as possible, why. And I couldn't do it without my brother's early memories of our family, because I had almost no memories of my own. He never got tired of answering my questions, even when I asked the same ones over and over again.

"Did I love her?" That was what disturbed me the most— not remembering her love for me, but mine for her.

"The last time we visited her in the hospital, you climbed into her bed, and it took two nurses to pull you away from her. You screamed all the way to the car."

I pictured a little girl who looked like me, clinging to her mother, holding on for dear life. I thought if I could remember that moment, remember loving someone that much, I'd be able to love like that again. "What did I say when she died?"

"You didn't understand. You kept asking me when she was coming back."

"What would you tell me?"

"I'd say, never. She's never coming back."

"You understood death?"

He'd pause. "I knew she wasn't coming back."

There was no laughter when we talked about our mother or what it was like before she died. We found nothing funny about those years. However, we laughed about everything else in our childhoods.

"Jean beat me with a belt once because I answered the telephone," I told my brother. Jean was my grandfather's second wife, and for a time I had lived with them in Baltimore. "She said twelve-year-olds had no business answering the telephone."

My brother and I would look at each other wide-eyed and laugh.

"I'd do anything to avoid being punished for wetting the bed," he'd say, "so I'd sleep sitting up in a chair and then wet the chair."

His bed-wetting stories could send us into hysterics. His wife and children would hear the laughter and return to the table.

"Tell us about the time you buried the suitcase full of dirty sheets," his daughter, Marguerite, would urge.

He'd tell us: a nine-year-old boy walks into the woods next to my grandmother's house carrying a suitcase containing a week's worth of urine-soaked sheets and buries it. Unbeknownst to him, the boy is followed by a servant. Later the servant digs up the suitcase and presents it to my grandmother while she and the boy are eating lunch. The boy is dragged from the table by his hair and locked in a bedroom

105

no one uses, with just a mattress on the floor. He is left there for a week with someone bringing his meals and letting him out to use the bathroom. At night he wets the mattress.

Why did we laugh? Why did the endless repetition of this repertoire of our childhood horrors strike us as so funny? We didn't laugh at the painful memories of others, just our own.

"We'd go nuts if we didn't laugh," my brother said.

"Hey, remember when they had our dog put to sleep and told us they had given her away?"

"Yeah, that was *really* funny."

What he said about Hank going through the Rolodex was more like being tripped than being handed a piece of Juicy Fruit, but it lessened some of the pressure I felt about having a date. If I wasn't someone special Hank had been losing sleep over for six years, I didn't have to live up to anything. I was just an R in the Rolodex after A through Q hadn't worked out. Maybe the Rs wouldn't either and he'd move on to the Ss. It gave me the courage to meet him.

As I stood in the kitchen, trying to absorb the idea that I had a date for the first time in almost ten years, the phone rang again. This time it was Allie. Before I could tell her about my date, she launched in about the horses. She said three days of letting the mares sniff each other over the stall door was plenty. Any longer and I'd be creating more tension by not allowing them to meet face to face. I should just turn them out in the pasture together. Right away.

"No lead lines," she said. "Just get out of the way and let them work it out."

"Lay Me Down is so stiff," I argued. "She won't be able to run if she needs to."

"Give her bute, wait an hour, and then let her out."

Bute is a painkiller and anti-inflammatory that comes as a white paste in an oral syringe. I gave Lay Me Down a moderate dose, waited an hour, and then it was time.

I decided to give Lay Me Down a head start, so I let her out first, hoping she'd wander to the far end of the pasture. She didn't, but she did go far enough to give her plenty of time to see Georgia coming. The bute had worked, and her gait was smoother, less labored. If she had to run, she could. Hotshot stood right next to her, and I wondered if he'd be a help or a hindrance. I knew he'd try to protect her, but he was old and no match for Georgia. Tempo grazed near the other two and my guess was that he wouldn't involve himself in whatever happened. He'd stay close and observe.

When I'd run out of reasons to delay the inevitable, I opened Georgia's door. If I hadn't moved to the side, she would have knocked me down. She left her stall at a dead run. I felt sick as I watched her gallop down the cement aisle and out of the barn. I ran after her to watch.

She went right for Lay Me Down, who had seen her coming and had trotted toward the far fence with Hotshot right behind her. Even with the bute, I could see Lay Me Down had trouble moving fast. Her trot looked stiff-kneed and choppy, the front legs worse than the rear. As a Standardbred, she should have easily been able to outrun a

Morgan but there had been so much damage to her joints from racing that she'd lost her advantage. At least her lungs were clear: she'd need all her breath.

Georgia's ears were flat back, and her neck was stretched out as far as a short, thick Morgan neck could stretch. At the end of her neck was her head with the lips curled back, exposing big, grass-stained teeth. She was moving so fast that all four feet were in the air at the same time. She looked like a TV trailer for a new reality show: *Killer Horses of Olivebridge*.

She reached Hotshot first—bless his poor, protective heart—and sank her teeth into his rump. He kind of kicked back but he was Hotshot; he didn't know how to be nasty, even in war. His kicks were no more than little bucks, his rear legs never getting farther off the ground than a few inches. Mostly they acted as body blocks and in that sense they sort of worked. He managed to keep Georgia from reaching Lay Me Down and, in the process, got bitten a lot.

This assault took place at a fairly high speed. All three horses were moving at a trot or a canter—four horses, if you counted Tempo, who circled at the periphery. The fight got closer and closer to the barn, and I wondered if Georgia was too far out of her mind to listen if I blocked the entry and yelled if she tried to get inside. I quickly fetched the buggy whip just in case. The sound of a cracking whip was the one thing that always got her respect.

Until then.

They were right up against the barn, everyone covered

in foamy sweat, their breathing fast and heavy. Georgia squealed as she kicked and bit, throwing one end of herself or the other at Lay Me Down. I lunged toward her, cracking the whip, shouting, "*NO*," and suddenly they were inside, the whip ignored.

Why hadn't I shut the door?

I never shut the two big sliding doors that hung on the overhead track. Not even in winter, when the wind and snow were howling, and it was below zero. For all I knew, after all these years, they'd rusted in that position and couldn't be shut. But I wished I had tried. I wished I'd thought of it. Lay Me Down and Georgia were inside now, going at each other, standing on the cement center aisle. Hotshot, Tempo, and I were outside, panting and scared.

The sound of metal horseshoes on cement is only pretty when it's slow and rhythmic, like when a horse walks in or out of the stall at feed time. This sound was different. This sounded like a car accident. They crashed against closed stall doors and hanging chains used for cross-tying horses when they were being groomed. They grunted and squealed and breathed as loud as humpback whales.

When I thought I couldn't stand another second, Lay Me Down fell onto the cement. Georgia came prancing out of the barn as proud as if she had just wiped out cholera. I went right to Lay Me Down, who was sitting dog style: front legs bent and tucked neatly to one side, her rear legs tucked to the same side. Her long neck rose straight up from her chest, her ears were forward and alert, listening for Georgia's return. I knelt at her side and checked all I could see of her for bites or wounds of any kind. She was wet and breathing hard, but she looked OK.

I ran my hand over her neck and back, talking to her softly, hoping she'd get up, but she didn't. It didn't feel right, her lying there like that. And the longer she lay there, the less right it felt. I went to the tack room to get her halter, and while I was up, I glanced outside to see where the others were. Georgia and Tempo were grazing together at the far end of the pasture, but Hotshot was standing right by the barn door. I noticed a few bare spots on his rump where Georgia had pulled out the hair, but otherwise he seemed to be in good shape.

I got Lay Me Down's halter and went back to where she was still lying and put it on. I gave her a few more minutes to compose herself, and then tried to get her up. *If I had shut the barn doors, this never would have happened.* The longer she lay there, the worse I felt.

I slipped the halter over her nose and ears and clipped on a lead line. I stood a few feet in front of her, leaving the lead line slack to see if she'd get up on her own. Most horses move forward as soon as they hear the snap of the lead line in place, but Lay Me Down didn't move.

"Come on, girl," I said and gave the line a little tug. When she still didn't move, I knelt next to her, pulling her head forward with one hand on her halter and pushing against her side with my shoulder. That worked. She heaved herself to her feet. Even on a good day, Lay Me Down got up with difficulty because of her overall stiffness. So, for a moment, it was hard to tell whether she was injured.

I led her down the aisle to see how she walked and that's when I noticed she was badly lame in one of her rear legs. She could hardly put any weight on it while walking, and when she stood, she held it up. I put her in her stall, pulled out the cell phone, and called the vet.

While I waited for the vet, I went to the house and got one of the sport wraps I kept in the freezer for my bad back and took it to the barn. I was pretty sure the injury was low in her leg, in the pastern, right above her hoof. She let me wrap the cold compress around it, and since I'd already given her bute, I didn't give her anything more for pain.

I offered her some hay and dried her down with a towel. She alternated between holding her foot up and letting just the tip of the hoof rest on the stall floor. I would have soaked it in cold water if I'd thought she'd have kept her foot in the bucket, but if she was going to keep pulling it out, the compress was better.

Dr. Grice arrived within the hour and drove her blue truck right up to the barn entrance. She was a tall young woman with short blonde hair, and the first vet none of my horses fled from. She was smart and gentle, a favorite with horse farms all over the Hudson Valley on both sides of the river.

I brought out Lay Me Down and cross-tied her in the center aisle on the flat cement floor where Dr. Grice could examine her and set up her portable X-ray machine, a square black box a little smaller than a toaster oven. When Dr. Grice took off the compress to examine the leg, we both saw Lay Me Down's pastern was already swollen, so icing it had been the right thing to do. I stood by Lay Me Down's head to keep her company while Dr. Grice put the injured leg through a range of motion series to confirm that the problem was in the pastern and not somewhere else. Whenever Dr. Grice touched near the pastern, Lay Me Down moved her head up and down and flicked her ears sideways, indicating her objection. Ears flat back would have shown more pain.

"I don't think it's broken," Dr. Grice said, "but we won't know for sure until we X-ray it."

We put what looked like a black rubber doormat under Lay Me Down's foot to help keep it level. Dr. Grice guided the injured leg down and placed it flat on the mat, but as soon as she moved away, Lay Me Down either picked up her foot or rested it, tilted, on the tip of her hoof. This went on for a while, and Dr. Grice finally said she'd take a picture with the hoof tilted and hope for the best.

She took several films from different angles, and when she was done, I put the cold compress back on Lay Me Down and led her into her stall. Dr. Grice gave Lay Me Down a shot of Banamine for pain and told me to continue giving her bute and applying the ice. She'd call with the results of the X-rays first thing in the morning.

I followed her out to her truck and found the other three horses standing around it, licking the hood. Big wet marks streaked the windshield and the side windows. At the back of the truck, where the flatbed would normally be, was a vet hospital on wheels, including running hot water. Doors swung open and bottles of medication, leg wraps, syringes, and stainless steel surgical tools slid out on long clean trays. It was a wonder of engineering and organization.

"Things should calm down now," Dr. Grice said, giving Georgia's mane an affectionate tug. She raised her eyebrows and looked right at Georgia.

Georgia gave her a sleepy blink as though it had just been another dull morning here at Ho-Hum Farm.

"*Mares,*" Dr. Grice said, shaking her head and patting the shiny red flank as she walked to the back of her truck to wash her hands.

I was so relieved she didn't hate Georgia, didn't single her out as being anything worse than "a mare." It was OK if I was angry, if I thought Georgia was a monster. She was *my* monster, my beloved Morgan monster. But I didn't want anyone else to think of her that way.

I followed Dr. Grice to the little water spigot at the back bumper and wondered why I felt so sensitive, as though if she said anything too nice or too mean, either way, I'd burst into tears, I who *never* cried. Maybe I was more upset about the two mares fighting than I realized. Maybe it was guilt for not closing the barn doors. I was so close to tears I knew that if she said anything but "Here's your bill," I'd cry.

She leaned over the spigot and soaped her hands and

arms, all the way to her elbows. "So," she said as she scrubbed, "how's everything going?"

I made it to the bumper near the spigot before the tears came. "Well," I squeaked in a tiny, clenched voice, "*I have this date.*"

[9]

ALL WEEK BEFORE my date I had trouble concentrating. During a counseling session at work I caught myself worrying about what to wear.

"You seem different," said my newly crack-free client. In the past he wouldn't have noticed if my chair was on fire.

"Different?"

"You didn't say anything about what's missing."

I yanked my attention away from myself and looked at the man on the other side of my desk. I felt exposed, found out. In his angry glare I saw that I was just another woman in a long line of women who didn't listen, who didn't care, who had failed him: his mother, his wife, his boss at work, who threatened to fire him if he didn't get treatment for his drug problem.

"You're right," I said. "I was distracted." I quickly looked

him over to see what was missing. Hair? Teeth? Nose? They
all seemed to be there. Limbs, digits, eyes. Everything was
there. "Missing?"

He sighed and patted the empty left breast pocket of his
shirt as though I'd missed the ax handle protruding from his
chest.

No cigarettes. "You quit!"

He rolled his eyes.

But he was right, I was different. After years of moth-
balling any need for a personal life, I found my upcoming
date with Hank had unleashed twin monsters of fear and
loneliness.

When Saturday arrived, I got up early to do barn chores.
Lay Me Down's pastern had not been broken but it was still
swollen and she was still lame. She was taking bute for pain
and swelling. While she ate her grain, I soaked her foot in
ice water.

She looked huge to me once again. I wasn't used to seeing her in a stall. She filled the twelve by fourteen-foot
space like a big doll in a small dollhouse. Her stall was diag-
onally across the aisle from Georgia's, in full sight. This was
good because they needed to get used to looking at each
other but bad because I felt disloyal whenever I was nice to
Lay Me Down in front of Georgia. I knew Georgia watched
me, and I knew she'd let me know how she felt sooner or
later: a nip, a shove, a step to my foot plus a little grinding.
She didn't forget.

I'd wait until Georgia was out of her stall and grazing

before I'd sneak Lay Me Down a hug. I felt like I was two-timing Georgia, an old and familiar feeling that had ended along with the Gallo wine. It wasn't who I was anymore: lying, making up stories about where I'd been, whom I'd been with, and what I'd been doing. It was hard to believe I'd ever been like that.

When Lay Me Down finished her grain, I lifted her foot out of the bucket and dried it before wrapping it in Vetrap, a wide elastic bandage that sticks to itself and is used to support the injured area of a horse's leg. I had chosen bright pink but it comes in every color imaginable. I guess people just like to add a splash of color to their horses to "accessorize" them.

Lay Me Down was fed, soaked, wrapped, drugged, and hugged, and then she was ready to join the herd. Hotshot waited patiently for her outside her stall door, ready to escort her to the pasture and to protect her against further attacks from Georgia. Fortunately, Georgia seemed to have gotten the worst of her rage out of her system. It was possible she felt she had made her point, established her alpha status. As long as Lay Me Down didn't get too close, Georgia left her alone. If she did get close, Georgia's ears flattened, and she rushed at Lay Me Down in warning.

Standing still, Lay Me Down was a work of art with long, graceful lines and muscle mass that exuded power. As soon as she moved, especially when she moved fast to get away from Georgia, she lost all her grace as she hobbled and lurched. She was truly and badly crippled. Bute helped but it can be hard on the stomach. A horse shouldn't stay on it indefinitely. I'd started adding arnica to her feed, a homeopathic treatment for pain that she could stay on for the rest of her life without any harmful side effects. But it was impossible to tell if the arnica was helping.

Early that same evening, after the second feed and before heading to the house to get ready for my date, I lingered at the fence a moment to watch the horses. Since Lay Me Down's arrival, they had remained in pairs. Hotshot and Lay Me Down grazed together, and Georgia and Tempo grazed at a distance from them. I'd yet to see Tempo and Lay Me Down together. Hotshot didn't permit it. I wondered if it would always be this way, this immutable division. I wondered what made a pair, what drew Hotshot to Lay Me Down so strongly, what drew anyone to anyone.

Something about the horses pairing off made me sad. Before Lay Me Down they'd been a group, a herd. Now they shut each other out. Sometimes a couple grazed so close together their noses touched, and it looked like they were telling secrets, whispering nasty things about the other couple, the way it felt sometimes when I was around couples at a dinner or a party—shut out of an exclusive club of two. I didn't have many friends who weren't married or living with someone, so I experienced this more often than I liked.

Now it was in my pasture. I stood at the fence and

watched the horse couples. It seemed to be the story of my life. It had been so long since I was part of a couple myself, it was as though I never had been, and in some ways I hadn't, not really. I don't think someone who drank the way I did was capable of being part of anything except in the most superficial way. I suspected real intimacy required more than intoxicated rambling no one remembered in the morning. I suspected it required something I couldn't even name but didn't think I possessed.

Oh, I liked being alone: having things my way, answering to no one, having the freedom to come and go. Yet when I talked to clients about their relationship or marital problems, I felt insincere. In my office at work I had a picture of Georgia and my deceased Newfoundland on my desk and had recently added a photograph of Lay Me Down. I knew for a fact I was the only person who worked at the agency who didn't have at least one photograph of a human being in her office. Clients noticed, too.

"No kids?" A young woman bent forward in her chair and squinted at the photographs of my animals.

"Well, actually, those are my children."

My response felt evasive, not because I thought women should have children or even because I thought I should, but because for me, it felt like unfinished business. It would have been more honest if I had said, "Ever since my mother died and my father left, I've been unable to get close to anyone."

I don't think men do this, reevaluate their lives, starting from birth, before going out to dinner with a woman.

Perhaps most women do not do this either but most women in their forties aren't dating.

Later, I stood in front of the full-length mirror in my bedroom, considering black jeans and a white T-shirt or black jeans and a black T-shirt. What was the right outfit for a date with a writer? Certainly not a skirt. I glanced at the pile on the bed. No, no, no. Why had I even pulled out the skirts?

Shoes? Clogs or the new Arche wedges I had cheered myself up with when I had (uncharacteristically) agreed to drive a friend to chemotherapy at Sloan-Kettering a few weeks ago? Clogs. Arches seemed pretentious. Best not to betray any sign of shallow, name-brand tendencies. This man probably liked women who didn't care about fashion, just books.

Earrings? The pearl dangles. I wore them every day, even with sweats. They gave just the right message: tasteful without being ostentatious, feminine without being girly, timeless without being fuddy-duddy.

Back to the T-shirt. I looked washed-out in white but black seemed a little hostile, like when I wasn't reading I was throwing down shots of tequila, lip-synching to Courtney Love. Better to stick with white even though it was slightly bridal.

Other jewelry? I liked real jewelry: oversized, chunky, and lots of it. Forget about quiet, tasteful, understated. Below the earlobes, the rules changed. It was my grandmother's fault. She liked a wrist shackled in precious metal and rocks, fingers that bulged with stones. Anything less than eighteen-karat gold was junk, and if you couldn't see the rocks, say, from across the dining room at the Colony Club, then they weren't worth wearing.

I tried dainty for a while: a slender gold bangle, a pinky ring with a ruby chip. It was what I could afford. But one day my grandmother gave me a few of her bracelets and a few of her necklaces. None of them were very valuable, but all of them were very big. After that I had to hold back.

I decided on a men's Swiss Army watch I could read without glasses and a wide gold cuff bracelet I'd worn almost every day for the past twenty years. Big but quiet; a compromise. No rings in case we shook hands.

Fifty minutes later, I was in the car on my way to meet Hank. I was accompanied by an Etta James CD, her big, soulful voice filling my car with the intensity I needed. When she sang "Let's Burn Down the Cornfield," something wild in me wanted to wear a thin dress and roll in the dirt with a man, wanted to set fire to whatever was holding me back. When the song was over, I hit *Replay*, and, after listening a few more times, I was ready for the next song, "Gonna Have Some Fun Tonight."

When I pulled into the parking lot at the restaurant, there was a bald man leaning against the trunk of his car. I knew he must be Hank, but I wouldn't have recognized him if I'd run into him on the street. He had changed, aged, which meant I had, too. It had been six years, of course we'd aged. Still, it was a shock.

He smiled and waved as I pulled my car next to his and parked. He wasn't quite bald. A neatly trimmed band of pale red circled the back of his head from ear to ear. The man I remembered was thin; this one was barrel-chested and plump.

He stood near my car door with his hands in his pockets, waiting for me to get out. I fumbled with the keys, my purse, the door handle. The dark, wild me had fled; it was the anxious, uptight me who got out of the car and extended a damp hand for him to shake. He ignored the hand, and I was pulled into the round belly and hugged hard. I must have been taller than he because I could feel his ear against my jaw.

He kept his hand on the small of my back as he guided me toward the restaurant. I tried to decide whether I liked being touched that way. His hand was light but it was there, as though it had a right to be. I thought, if I were Lay Me Down, I'd be flicking my tail about now. I'd be asking Hotshot to back off.

Inside there were white linen tablecloths, candles, and the sound of chamber music. The dining area was one large room divided into smaller sections by waist-high wooden partitions filled with plants. The rug was dark green with little maroon fleurs-de-lis. French windows were draped with matching velvet curtains, left open to views of fields and woods. We followed a maître d' in a black tuxedo through the buzz of muffled voices to our table in a quiet corner.

I took my first really good look at him when we were seated across the small table from one another. He had that pale, freckly skin redheads have. He plucked a bread stick from the bread basket and took a bite. Crumbs fell all over the table, but he didn't notice or didn't care, and he took another bite. More crumbs fell. He was wearing a gray T-shirt and a blue blazer that now had crumbs on the lapels. He brushed at his front halfheartedly but most of the crumbs remained. He seemed utterly relaxed.

I was just this side of whispering the Twenty-third Psalm. It seemed easier to die than date. It was too hard, too much effort, requiring too many things I didn't have: youth, small talk, great underwear.

"Do you like wine?" he asked, picking up the wine list.

Another reason I shouldn't have come. How did I explain this? "I don't drink," I said.

He poked his head out from behind the wine list. "Nothing?" Pale red eyebrows shot into the middle of his forehead.

"Nothing."

He put the wine list down near the edge of the table. "Then neither will I."

It was the first thing about him I liked. He didn't ask questions, didn't probe, and then abstained to keep me company. At least I thought it was to keep me company. As it turned out, it was the last thing I liked about him as well. The rest of the evening was pretty much downhill, beginning with the news that he was only separated from his wife, not divorced.

We ordered and the food came. He ate with gusto, I picked. I was too nervous to eat. He wasn't handsome but he was intelligent, with a sense of humor. When I took my jacket off, he looked me over. I looked him over, too, all through dinner. I was trying to decide if he was someone I could sleep with. Not tonight, but sometime. I thought maybe I could. I wasn't sure. I wasn't sure of anything.

"I haven't had a date in ages," I said.

He didn't even look up from his steak. "Is that what this is, a date?"

I felt like I'd just sneezed on his food, made a faux pas, calling this a date. But, yes, I thought it was.

When he finally looked up, he noticed the unfinished piece of salmon on my plate. "Are you going to eat that?"

"Help yourself," I said and pushed my plate toward him. Watching him eat my dinner was like feeling his hand on my back all over again. It made me want to pull away, tell him he didn't know me well enough for that. He'd been married for twenty years, I reminded myself. He knew as little about dating as I did.

"I'd like something sweet," I said after he'd finished eating my salmon.

Hank held his hand up to signal the waiter. "I'm not a sugar eater myself."

When the dessert menu came, I ordered something called Death by Chocolate. It felt like a prophecy.

"My daughter doesn't eat sugar either," Hank said and ordered herbal tea.

"Are you working on a book?" I asked.

"A book?" He frowned. "I haven't written a book in five years."

His grievances included the extinction of good editors, good publishers, and good money.

"I don't even read," he added.

He didn't read? This surprised me more than his not writing. Who didn't read? I got an image of a glowing television set, hot as molten steel, turned to the Sports Channel for five years straight.

But what really bothered me was his tone of voice. It was dismissive, mocking, the way some people talked about the religion of others, as though there was something desperate and childish about believing in a God or an afterlife. His tone said writing and reading books were OK for the little people, but the enlightened were investing in strip malls, like Hank and his small group of partners.

"We fly over rural and suburban areas and look for potential sites—a field, an abandoned drive-in. When we see something, we buy it, develop it, and lease it. Whole thing takes less than a year, from spotting the site to cutting the ribbon on opening day. We have about seventy malls, all the way from Texas to the Canadian border."

I was with a man who was cementing over America, bringing Blockbuster into the lives of book haters everywhere. It was like expecting to meet Charles Frazier for dinner and having someone wearing a Century 21 blazer with a pocketful of real estate brochures show up.

I didn't know what to say. As a group, I put writers on the same level as horses: a species almost beyond reproach. Whatever their imperfections, they were still writers. They got me through my childhood, through the last ten years without a date. Whatever sanity I had was thanks to writers, to books that either helped me forget my troubles or helped me understand them. I was one of those people who thought the answer to everything was in a book. To me, the phone book was a book. I could hardly believe we got it free.

My dessert arrived and Hank's herbal tea. The cake was such a slender wedge, I was surprised it had remained upright on its journey from the kitchen. I took a bite and understood the small portion. It was incredibly rich.

"Delicious," I reported to the sugar hater.

He picked up his spoon and let it hover over my plate. "May I?"

"Sure." I nudged the plate in his direction.

He pulled the plate over until it was right in front of him, then he cut the cake in half with his spoon and shoved the whole piece into his mouth. While he chewed, he didn't push the plate back toward me, so I put my fork down and pretended. *What chocolate cake? What hypocrite of a sugar-hating nonwriter?*

"Like it?" I asked, as he took another bite of the piece that was left on my plate.

He shoved the plate away and wiped his mouth with a napkin. The bottom half of his face was contorted as though he'd just sucked a lemon. "Terrible," he said, picking up his cup and gulping tea. "I can already feel a canker sore." He traced the inside of his lip with his tongue.

For this man I had lost sleep? I had wept in front of my vet? Had torn my bedroom apart looking for something with lace to wear? For this man I had become daring and courageous, a Christopher Columbus rat?

I stared at the remaining morsel of cake. "What happens when you like something?"

He shook his head, still chewing, still hunting for that canker sore with his tongue. "It's not the taste," he said. "Did you know that sugar is the primary cause for the dumbing down of America? For turning everyone into zombies?"

"I thought not reading was," I said.

"Nope. Sugar." He smiled. "I feel dumber already; how about you?"

It was the first time he'd smiled all night, and his smile was nice. It changed his whole face, made him seem sexy, like someone who'd like to lick chocolate off my toes. Then I thought of all the time I'd wasted being nervous about this date, about whether this man would like me.

"I don't need sugar to feel dumb," I said.

"You? Dumb?" Still smiling, he shook his head. "I don't date dumb women. Only smart, pretty ones."

Maybe it was a line but I fell for it. Still, I couldn't help it. He'd made me suffer too long. "Is that what this is," I asked, "a date?"

"Touché." He smiled and leaned over to spear the last bite of cake.

[10]

WEEK AFTER my date, Allie stopped by early on a Saturday morning before the bugs were bad. We stood at the fence with our coffee watching my four horses. They were still two separate couples, but now the pairs were grazing closer together, the geldings always positioned between the mares.

"She looks so good," Allie said about Lay Me Down's recovery. She was still limping from Georgia's attack, but the Vetrap was gone, and she was on the mend. Gone, too, was the dull coat, the hacking cough, the skin with open sores stretched over protruding bones. She looked as sleek and brown as a Hershey bar, as sweet as one, too.

As if she knew we were talking about her, Lay Me Down stopped grazing and walked over to the fence where Allie and I stood. She came up to us and sighed into Allie's cup.

Allie spilled a little coffee into the palm of her hand and let Lay Me Down lick it up.

"Stingy," I said, watching the big tongue search for more in the emptied palm.

"OK, OK," she said and let Lay Me Down lick it right out of the cup.

As Lay Me Down lapped coffee, Allie looked at her in that funny way she looked at people when she was trying to figure out something. It made me nervous.

"What?" I chewed my bottom lip.

"When was the last time you had the vet here?"

"A week ago. After the fight with Georgia."

"Look at her eyes," Allie said.

I looked. They were big and brown with enormous black eyelashes. They were beautiful. "What about them?"

"They're not the same," she said.

I looked again. They seemed exactly the same to me.

"The right eye protrudes more than the left." She pointed at it.

Horse eyes protrude. All of them. That's the way horses are made. Lay Me Down's looked normal to me. But this was Allie talking, and she looked concerned.

"Are you saying something's wrong?"

Allie studied Lay Me Down for a few more minutes. "See if you can get the vet to come today," she said.

My heart skipped a beat. I gripped my coffee cup with sweaty fingers. I was torn between wanting to ask more and telling her to shut up. I hurried inside to call. Jeannie, the

woman who ran the office, answered. She was knowl-
edgeable about horses so I told her what Allie had said
about the eye protruding. All five vets at the clinic knew
Allie, and they knew she wouldn't have asked for someone
to come that quickly if there wasn't a good reason. Dr.
Grice was on call and could get to my place sometime in
the afternoon. I wished that I knew a human doctor's office
that was run as well and caringly as Rhinebeck Equine. If
you needed them, they came, day or night.

When I went back outside, Lay Me Down had finished
Allie's coffee and had returned to the herd to graze. We
stayed at the fence a few more minutes before Allie had to
leave.

"It might be nothing," she said, brushing flyaway hairs off
her forehead. Her fingers were smooth and muscular from
years of giving massages with oils. After they brushed away
the hair, her fingers traced the length of the still-neat braid
falling forward over her shoulder.

"You never wear your wedding ring," I remarked.

She held up her bare left hand, fanning out the fingers
and rubbing the joints. They ached, a result of advanced
Lyme disease, something she'd had for over fifteen years.
Sometimes the stiffness would become so painful and
debilitating that she'd go back on antibiotics for several
weeks to kill off some of the spirochetes. "Did what's-his-
name call yet?" she asked, massaging her sore hands. She
meant Hank.

"What a jerk," I said, shaking my head.

Most of my friends thought I was the jerk, however, Allie included. They thought I was judging Hank unfairly, being hasty. When I said it bothered me that he'd put his hand on my back and then eaten most of my dinner, they looked at me like they were still waiting to hear the annoying part.

That's just men.

Men like food.

Men always talk about themselves.

Strip malls? At least he has money.

"You should call him," Allie said.

"He told me he's allergic to most animals. *Especially* horses."

She turned and scrutinized me the same way she had just scrutinized Lay Me Down. She sighed and shook her head.

I would not call this man. It would have meant admitting that I wanted this man, whom I didn't like, to like me. We'd had dinner and he'd never called. Despite my feelings, I wanted him to want me. I already felt abandoned. The scary part was, this made perfect sense to me.

"He's not even divorced," I said.

She gave me a look. "A technicality. Give him another chance." She started walking toward her car. "Call me later. Tell me what the vet says."

After she left, I went to the barn to get a halter for Lay Me Down. While I was putting it on, I looked at her eyes again, comparing them. I still saw no difference, none whatsoever. She sighed as I snapped shut the cheek latch and waited for me to indicate what we were going to do next. I stroked her neck and then gently pushed her away to let her know we weren't going anywhere, she could go back to grazing.

I would have petted her more, scratched along her neck, her belly, the top of her withers, all the places she loved to be scratched. But I couldn't, not in front of Georgia. Giving Lay Me Down more than a few minutes of attention was all it took to bring Georgia trotting across the pasture looking for a fight.

After lunch, I shut all four horses in their stalls and opened the pasture gate so Dr. Grice could drive right up to the barn. Forty-five minutes later, her blue truck stopped in front of the barn entrance. This time her assistant was with her, a young woman named Donna, who waved hello before she got out of the truck. I waved back from where I stood, just inside the entrance. I was always apprehensive when the vet came, and this time I was too nervous to make small talk.

"Thanks for coming," I said when they got out of the truck. "Do you want her inside or out?" Inside, there was more control over the horse; outside, there was better light. Dr. Grice knew it was going to be an eye exam because Jeannie had told her about my earlier call.

"Let's start inside," she said, walking toward the entrance where I stood with my arms crossed, hoping I didn't look as nervous as I felt.

I opened Lay Me Down's stall door and followed Dr.

Grice and Donna to the end of the aisle. Lay Me Down seemed curious about her visitors but not anxious. While she sniffed the two newcomers, I snapped a lead line on her halter and waited to be told what to do.

"Allie thinks it's the right eye?" Dr. Grice asked, already widening the opening of Lay Me Down's right eye with her thumb and forefinger and looking into it. Lay Me Down let her examine it without pulling away. The assistant stood on the other side, scratching Lay Me Down's neck and mumbling soothing words.

Dr. Grice didn't offer any preliminary opinions, and I didn't ask. She spent a few minutes looking into each eye, then did it a second time. When she was done, she wiped her hands on a towel and looked thoughtful.

"We'll do a sonogram on the right eye," she said. "It does seem to be protruding. We'll set it up right here. The light's good enough."

I wanted to leave, hide in the house until this was over and Dr. Grice was gone. Instead, I nodded and, as I waited while they went back to the truck for whatever they needed, I stood next to Lay Me Down and scratched her neck. She leaned into my hand, into the scratch, letting me know the places she liked. Her trust in me felt awful. I had brought her to my farm to be safe but she wasn't. I was helpless against a protruding eye.

They came back with all kinds of supplies, most of which Donna carried in a stainless-steel bucket. Dr. Grice had a stethoscope around her neck and carried a small box

in her arms that turned out to be the ultrasound machine.
They put everything down on the cement floor, and we let
Lay Me Down sniff as much of it as she wanted because if
horses are allowed to sniff new things, they are less afraid.
(Not Tempo. He was afraid of everything and became more
fearful if you let him sniff, especially if it was medical.
With Tempo, the trick was speed and, if that didn't work,
a tranquilizer shot.)

The only thing I'd ever seen Lay Me Down afraid of was
Georgia, but Georgia was locked in her stall so Lay Me Down
seemed relaxed. She sighed over the bucket and licked the lid
of the sonogram machine. Everything she did seemed precious to me, precious and tender. For me, her terrible past was
always a presence, a reminder of what it was that had survived: this sweet, kind nature, qualities so lacking in my
human family they seemed like miracles to me now.

Before she did the sonogram, Dr. Grice listened to Lay
Me Down's heart and lungs and pronounced them both
strong and healthy: I had a moment of elation, of crazy
hope. How sick could a horse be with a good heart and
clear lungs? Next she gave her a tranquilizer shot because,
even though she was calm and good-natured, the tranquilizer would help keep the eye from blinking when the sonogram wand touched it.

While we waited for the shot to take effect, Dr. Grice
set up her equipment. The ultrasound machine was a metal
cube, half the size of a briefcase, with a long cord attached
to a smooth wand on the end. There was a second small box

attached to the first. This was the printer that would print out the image of Lay Me Down's eye. No waiting. In a few minutes we'd know why this eye protruded.

We knew the tranquilizer had taken effect when Lay Me Down let her head drop a foot or so closer to the floor. She blinked slowly, sighed slowly, and she'd forgotten she had a tail. It hung off her rump as limp as laundry. I stood to the left of her head, holding her halter so Dr. Grice had access to the eye on the right. I would have liked a little of whatever was in Lay Me Down's shot.

"Can you lift her head?" Dr. Grice asked.

"Come on, Lay Me Down," I said, cradling her head in my arms and urging it upward an inch or two. Her head was heavy, she was sleepy. I liked having the giant head in my arms. Under normal conditions, it would never have been possible to snuggle a horse like that.

"Right there," Dr. Grice said when the eye was at our shoulder level. She snapped on a pair of latex gloves and squeezed some clear gel onto her fingers. She held Lay Me Down's sleepy eye open with one hand, and, with the other, spread the gel all over it. Lay Me Down didn't blink at all. When the eye was coated, Dr. Grice's assistant handed her the wand, and, right away, Dr. Grice started moving the smooth, round end over the surface of the slippery eye.

It seemed to take no time at all, less than five minutes, before the little printer began chattering. It printed out several separate images. From where I stood, they looked like

dirty smudges. Dr. Grice finished and handed the wand to
her assistant.

"Let me take a look at the printouts before we put her
back in the stall," she said. "If they're not clear, we may need
to repeat some."

She took off her gloves and knelt by the printer. The barn
was so quiet. The only sounds were the horses eating hay
and the swallows scolding us in high-pitched cries as they
swooped in and out, tending their nests, one in every stall,
right on top of the light fixture. A swallow roommate for
each horse. Sometimes I wondered if they got the same
roommates year after year. I worried about fire but
couldn't bring myself to destroy the nests. Mostly they
were made of mud, but tendrils of horse tail and straw hung
down, forming little lamp shades of debris around the
bare bulbs.

"You can put Lay Me Down back in her stall," Dr. Grice
said. "The pictures are nice and clear."

I knew something was wrong because of what Dr. Grice
didn't say. She didn't say, *Everything's OK*. Wobbly-kneed
with anxiety, I led Lay Me Down back to her stall slowly.
She was too sedated to go any faster. I slipped off her halter with shaky hands, gave her a pat, and left her dozing
until the drug wore off.

Dr. Grice and her assistant were standing in the barn entry
where the light was good, studying the sonograms. I joined
them, looking over Dr. Grice's shoulder at the lines and
smears on the the piece of paper in her hand. She started to talk

about the eye, pointing at the different blotches and telling me what they were, what they did, how an eye worked. I was listening but I wasn't, partly because no matter what she pointed at, I saw nothing recognizable. The smudges and lines weren't even in the shape of an eye. They were scattered across the paper in no pattern meaningful to me.

The other reason I wasn't attending was because I was really only listening for one word. The one word in all the medical jargon that I'd understand, that would communicate to me exactly what we were in for. Not just in the medical sense, maybe least of all in the medical sense. Were we climbing or falling? Was there a way out or not?

She started to say words I understood. Not the word I was looking for, but close cousins. Tumor. Mass. Growth. Then she said the word. She said *cancer*. She said it might or it might not be cancer. She said it wasn't someplace we could biopsy. It was too dangerous, too many blood vessels and optic nerves. There was no telling how deep it was, how far into her brain it might already be. She kept referring to the printout, to different parts of the smudge, but I wasn't really looking. Not even when she pointed right to the mass, to the tumor, and said, "See, it's this whole area. The readout is very clear."

What was clear to me was we were falling. I didn't know how fast but we were falling. And what I wanted to know was, what did the way down look like.

"Well," Dr. Grice said, chosing her words carefully, "I don't know. She could have a month, six months, a year, even two. Depends how fast this grows and what parts of the brain it affects."

There were sure to be neurological horrors I had never considered. There might be seizures, for instance, a thousand pounds of twitching, thrashing horse. There might be dementia, frenzy, paralysis. My mother died blind, paralyzed, and wasted. I didn't remember it but I had seen her, I had been there. The memory was in me somewhere. It came out here, in this barn with Dr. Grice, as I learned how sick this horse was, what might happen, and realized how scared I was and how helpless.

Dr. Grice would send the sonogram results to the veterinary hospital at Cornell for a second opinion, to a vet there who specialized in eye tumors. Maybe he'd suggest a treatment protocol other than wait and see. I asked her for a copy of the printouts to send to a homeopathic vet in Florida I used sometimes. I didn't know what he would say about the tumor but his treatment approach was nontraditional, noninvasive, and holistic. I'd never met him but had had several lengthy phone consultations with him over the past ten years. In the back of my mind I was thinking about pain management.

I tried to imagine what it would feel like to have something pressing against my eye hard enough to make it protrude. "Does her eye hurt?" I asked. Did horses get headaches?

Dr. Grice didn't think she was in pain. Lay Me Down might have felt some pressure but not pain, not yet. However, there would be signs to watch for, signs of discomfort: if she held her head at a strange angle, rubbed her eye or forehead against her leg, didn't eat, swung her head from side to side, any behavior that was outside the norm for this horse, anything at all.

"Could this have been caused by the way she was treated?" I asked as I walked Dr. Grice out to her truck. "From being hit around the eyes and head?" Even as I asked, I realized it made no difference. It wouldn't help us to save her.

"We don't know what causes these eye tumors," she said as she washed her hands. Her assistant was pulling out drawers and cabinets, putting away the sonogram machine and printer and emptying the contents of the stainless-steel bucket they had carried into the barn. Then she pulled out a flat aluminum box that held medical forms and also acted as a writing desk and began writing up my bill.

One of the reasons Dr. Grice was so well liked was that she always left you with hope. Not insincere, pie-in-the-sky hope, but real hope. She did it now.

"The eye cavity is big. It could be a long time before she can't shut her eye. Until then, she should feel OK."

"What do we do when she can't shut her eye?" A horse had to be able to blink to keep its eyes moist.

"Let's see what Dr. Rebhun at Cornell says. This is his area of expertise." Dr. Grice was sitting sideways in the cab of her truck, her knees facing out with the writing desk on her lap that Donna had passed to her so Dr. Grice could finish writing up the bill. As she talked, she was sketching a horse head and an eye. Then she drew a circle to show where the tumor was.

In a few minutes she'd pull out of my driveway, leaving me behind with the terrible question that would confront me every morning. What would the eye look like today? How it looked would determine everything else. It would tell us if she was in pain, how fast we were falling, if we'd hit bottom. I felt like tugging at Dr. Grice's pant leg and saying, "Wait a minute, let me find a grown-up, somebody to be in charge."

It was the way I had felt as a new social worker the first time a patient told me he wanted to commit suicide. I wanted to run out of the room and get help, find the person who would know what to do, tell Mommy.

Facing my frightened, helpless self was the hardest part about a crisis, especially a medical one. Before I did anything else, I had to grapple with overwhelming feelings of self-doubt and denial. Maybe everyone has to deal with those feelings, I don't know. I just know that I did not feel well equipped for what I was facing now. My first instinct when Dr. Grice started talking had been to put my hands over my ears and yell, *Stop!* Then when she mentioned the word *tumor*, a voice in my brain immediately said, *Maybe she's never done a sonogram, maybe she's reading it upside down.* Then when I finally absorbed what she had told me, when I was no longer questioning or blaming the messenger, I was clobbered with anxiety.

I doubted Dr. Grice saw any of this. And why should she?

My model for behavior was the Dalai Lama, because he smiled no matter what. When I was little, my model had been the Queen of England because she exhibited no feelings whatsoever except a love of horses. Most of the time I achieved a blend. Call it cheerful reserve or quiet strength. *Boy,* I wanted people to think, *there goes a calm woman.*

There was that little incident of weeping on Dr. Grice's bumper over a dinner date with a man, but I didn't do that very often, and I was sure Dr. Grice had been surprised, just as she would have been surprised to know how alone and afraid I felt now, how incompetent.

I stood by the truck, squinting into the impossibly beautiful afternoon, trying to fit the word *tumor* into the kaleidoscope of spring surrounding me. It was a bad word to float across verdant pastures bordered by flowering orchards. How had it found its way down this country lane on to my small farm tucked behind its sturdy fence? It was like the word *death* finding its way into Christmas, the last day I'd seen my mother alive. Where, in the cluster of gifts underneath the Christmas tree, did you put a dead mother?

Dr. Grice had finished writing my bill, and the corner of the paper fluttered in the breeze as she held it out to me. "She's a lucky horse," she said, "because you'll take such good care of her."

I smiled and nodded even though I knew she was wrong. I knew somehow I'd run away.

[11]

$\mathcal{L}$ AY ME DOWN'S illness filled me with a sense of urgency. It changed time from something abstract to something almost visible, something to be watched and measured, something as precious as Lay Me Down herself. Time was achingly finite and unfair, too. Lay Me Down deserved better. So had my mother. And what about me?

I started to dread going to the barn in the morning. I used to wake up with a feeling of pleasant anticipation at the thought of morning chores, at starting the day with horses. Watching Lay Me Down's eye changed that. Within a few weeks, the eye had protruded enough for me to see how different it was from the healthy eye. Now when I woke up, I crept to the window, half expecting to see Lay Me Down weaving her head in pain or lying dead next to a grieving Hotshot.

For several weeks after the diagnosis, I considered euthanizing her immediately. Why put her through another ordeal? Why put me through it? Then I'd go to the barn and feed her, brush her, spend time with her, and the truth is, she was content. I'd even say she was happy.

She did something all horses do but when she did it, it seemed different to me, as though she got a special enjoyment out of it. Early in the morning, when the sun was just up and the bugs weren't out yet, she'd find the spot where the sun first hit the pasture and sunbathe. All my horses loved the morning sun but Lay Me Down was always there first and sunbathed the longest. Maybe she loved the sun because she was more sensitive to cold or maybe because once she had been kept inside and didn't see the sun for a year. When it became too hot for the other three, and they'd gone back to the barn, Lay Me Down would stand in the sun another thirty or forty minutes, then have a good roll before going inside. And in the end, that's why I decided not to euthanize her: because she loved the sun.

Once I decided to see Lay Me Down through her illness, something in me changed. The dread I felt about morning chores went away, and I felt less apprehensive, less scared. I spent more time with her. I talked to the homeopathic vet in Florida and he sent me a super vitamin concoction to help boost her immune system. He also sent me a liquid remedy that might slow the growth of the tumor or even shrink it. I put a few drops of it in her grain every day, along with her vitamins, carrots, and—thanks to Allie—a candy peppermint. My grandmother had instilled in me a strict no-sugar rule for horses that had lasted thirty years, until the day Allie heard about it. "That's ridiculous," she'd said and brought my horses their first bag of peppermints. Lay Me Down always carefully picked the peppermint out of her grain bucket and ate it first.

I was particularly diligent about fly proofing her. I didn't want a single fly near her face, especially near her bad eye. I used Avon's Skin So Soft straight from the bottle, dabbing it around her eye with a cotton ball. I coated the inside of her ears with Bag Balm, originally made for cows but a good antiseptic salve for all animals. I sprayed the rest of her with a strong commercial horse spray. I didn't like using conventional horse sprays because they contained such toxic chemicals, but they worked better at keeping flies away, and with Lay Me Down, it was crucial to keep her bad eye free from infection. If the eye continued to push out, she'd wear a full-head fly hood made of nylon mesh.

To further reduce flies, I kept her stall extra clean and bought cedar chips instead of pine shavings for her bedding. Cedar was twice as expensive but made the whole barn smell nice and probably helped reduce the flies in everyone's stall. When they got really bad in the middle of the summer, I shut Lay Me Down in her stall while I was at work and put a box fan in her window set on low so she'd always have a breeze. Keeping her in her stall was to ensure that she would never be trapped outside the barn by Georgia. The arrangement seemed to make everyone happy, including Lay Me Down, who headed right for her stall when she saw me walking across the pasture in the morning. I left hay for Georgia and Tempo in their stalls and put Hotshot's right outside Lay Me Down's door, because as far as I could tell, that's where he spent the day.

There was a young woman I occasionally hired to take care of my horses when I was away. Hannah had grown up around horses and still had one of her own, though she had less time to ride since beginning a business program at the nearby community college earlier that fall. Because I didn't know what symptoms Lay Me Down might develop, I was nervous about leaving her alone all day. I decided to call Hannah to see if she could check on Lay Me Down while I was at work.

"She seems OK right now," I told her, "but soon she might need meds or some kind of dressing." But that wasn't my worst fear. "She could have a seizure," I added, cringing at the image of Lay Me Down thrashing around helplessly on the floor of her stall. I held my breath, expecting Hannah to politely decline. Who in their right mind would want to take on the responsibility of an animal this sick?

"Sure," she said without hesitating. "I can stop by almost anytime. Most of my classes are at night."

"*Thank you,*" I breathed, more relieved than I could express. We agreed I would pay her ten dollars an hour, more if and when Lay Me Down needed some kind of treatment. For now, Hannah would clean her stall, change her water, and give her fresh hay and a treat.

As the summer wore on, I was less fearful, but I was sadder, too, and softer somehow. The mornings I spent in the barn before work seemed precious and too short. One morning I found my Siamese cat sitting on the sunny windowsill of Georgia's stall, Georgia below with her neck stretched toward him, taking a cautious sniff. She knew about cat claws, and the sight brought tears to my eyes. Because it was funny? Sweet? Ironic that a fourteen-pound cat commanded this kind of respect from Georgia when no one else did?

It was as if in accepting Lay Me Down's illness I'd accepted something else, something bigger. I had thought I would prepare for her death by pulling back, withholding my feelings, or even euthanizing her before any symptoms developed. Instead, I spent more time with her.

She was the only horse I resumed grooming daily, and she loved the attention. I'd wait until she'd finished her grain and then bring the grooming kit in and set it on the floor, where she'd sigh over it as if greeting a long-lost foal. I'd pull out the curry comb with the dull rubber teeth and, starting high on her neck, brush in short, vigorous circles, loosening dead skin and dirt from one end of her to the other. The harder I brushed, the better she liked it, bobbing her head and leaning into the brush whenever I came to a particularly itchy spot. When I was done currying and her whole body was covered in the dirty little circles a curry comb leaves, I'd get out the red brush with the long nylon bristles and brush away all the loosened dirt, leaving her coat soft and shiny. I'd brush out her short dark mane, which never seemed to grow, and get the worst tangles out of her tail with my hands, leaving the real tail brushing for the weekends when I had more time. When I was done, I'd fly proof her, give her a second peppermint, turn on her fan, and leave her fresh hay and water for the day. In the evening when I got home from work, I'd repeat the routine, only then I'd open her stall door and let her out to graze with the other three horses in the cooler air of the relatively insect-free night.

The more time I spent with her, the sadder I sometimes felt, but I didn't pull back. I just felt sad. Animals live in the moment, and that's what I tried to do that summer, getting up half an hour earlier in order to spend more time with all four of my horses but especially with Lay Me Down. In a way I felt more alive, filled with the smells of summer: the sweet new hay in the hayloft, the woodsy smell of cedar chips, the heady perfume of the wild roses growing along the stone wall near the barn, and Lay Me Down's peppermint breath.

In the middle of July, Hank called. His message took up the whole answering-machine tape with an apology for not calling sooner and a monologue about ugly divorce details that I fast-forwarded through to the end, where he asked if I'd like to have dinner. Afterward I sat by the phone, staring at the answering machine, drawing starbursts on the message pad, a wide smile stretched across my face.

Before I called him back, before I even knew if I'd see

him again, I headed straight to Victoria's Secret in the Hudson Valley Mall. It was a knee-jerk reaction, a sense that it was time to change something. At the store I chose seven pairs of black lace, French-cut bikini panties.

"No pretty bra to match?" asked the child behind the counter, smiling. This was something I hadn't even considered. "Can I leave these here?" I asked, dropping the underwear on the counter as I headed for the bras.

"I'm Trudy, if you need help," she chirped.

Did Trudy think I needed help getting into a bra? I looked around. There were no women in their forties in sight. I told myself I was lucky I had a figure that still looked OK in this sort of thing. I *assumed* it looked OK. I hadn't actually tried anything on yet. But if I planned ahead, if I bought enough of the right thing in the right size, I'd never have to come back again as long as I lived. I'd never again have to be the only woman in Victoria's Secret who was old enough to be Trudy's grandmother.

Suddenly I felt really old, old and crazy. Maybe that's how Trudy saw me. When I left, she and the other size-two clerk would laugh about the crone who'd just bought all those giant-sized black bikinis. "Think she still does it?" they'd ask.

That's what I wanted to know when I was that age, who still did it. I would have assumed women of my age didn't because who'd want them? They were old. I remembered being twenty-four at a friend's twenty-fifth birthday party and feeling like a big wall had just dropped between us. She was old and I wasn't. The difference between our ages was only a few months but it might as well have been decades. It was all over for her. People twenty-five and up just sat around waiting to die. That was what I'd thought.

So while I was waiting to die, I looked at bras. The last thing on my mind was comfort. It seemed to be the last thing on Victoria's Secret's mind, too. It was the land of the underwire, a place where breasts were something to be worn just under the chin. At the moment I was willing to go along with that. I wouldn't have been in there if I hadn't been.

I wasn't sure of my size. Smallish. The kind of shape that in the past had made men say, "I *prefer* flat women." I bet they did, the way I preferred men with no teeth. Still, the As had less to fear from gravity. They also had less to choose from, which wasn't so bad considering there were four big walls covered with bras on little plastic hangers. It was the kind of thing that flooded me with anxiety. There were too many choices. It was why I didn't like to shop in department stores like Bloomingdale's and Macy's. To find one skirt you had to look through a thousand? *Why?* It was a maze and a house of horrors all in one. No matter where you turned, as far as the eye could see, you bumped into skirts.

For me, shopping boiled down to getting it over with quickly, so I selected a few black bras, a few white ones, and headed for the dressing room. From four walls of bras to four walls of mirrors, it was a toss-up which was worse. The good news was that I was working with the half of my body where lying to myself about cellulite wouldn't be necessary. There was the *Cellulite is beautiful* lie, the *Babies have cellulite, too, and they're cute* lie, and the whopper of them all, only possible in certain kinds of lighting, *It's gone!*

I tried not to look in the mirror until I had to, which wasn't easy in a tiny room lined with mirrors. By mistake I glimpsed myself in my own bra, the one I had worn from home. It reminded me of the Timex watch ad where they strap a Timex to the bottom of someone's ice skate and then run over it with a bulldozer and then dig it out of the sand a year later, smashed and filthy, but still ticking. That was my bra, a grayish film stuck to my skin that looked like something I should exfoliate. If Trudy saw me now, she'd run for a Ziploc bag and tweezers.

I shoved the old bra into the front pocket of my jeans, horrified I'd let myself come to this. It was as though, surrounded by all these mirrors, I couldn't escape seeing the part of my life I'd buried. So often I felt a kind of smug satisfaction in my independence, the poster girl for living alone and loving it. I wasn't single, I was autonomous. I was free. I was that fish without a bicycle. I was complete.

So why did I feel like weeping into the pretty lace bras? Why did all this freedom suddenly seem so awful? Poor Hank. Poor any man who made a date with such an ambivalent woman. But right now it wasn't ambivalence I was feeling; it was gaping, shrieking loneliness.

It wasn't what I'd expected would happen to me at Victoria's Secret. I had come for underwear, not insight, but

I'd gotten both. The underwire principle of life: make the most of what you've got. It did wonders for my body; why not for the rest of me?

I was ready to pay for my new life, which was heaped on the counter in a small pile of black and white lace. Trudy sorted through it, scanning in the prices, murmuring little sounds of approval as though she suspected I was doing something out of character and wanted to encourage it. When she was done ringing everything up, she didn't hit *Total*. Instead, she looked at me and frowned. "Having the wrong nightie could spell disaster." Her expression was dead serious, as though a problematic nightie was on a par with other global threats: war, famine, the hole in the ozone.

"A nightie?" I felt exposed. I'd been caught with a half-baked plan to end loneliness. I couldn't escape yet.

"Follow me," she said and headed across the store to a rack of nighties. She turned around to consider me from head to foot and then turned back to study the rack. She pulled out a diaphanous forest green garment that might have been a slip and held it up to me. "I like real silk, don't you?"

I took the nightie from her and held it up to myself, turning to face a mirror. "Now I do," I said.

My second dinner with Hank was nothing like the first. This time there was a sexual tension between us that gave the whole night a pleasant incoherence. Nothing much about him bothered me—not the crumbs on his lapel, the strip malls desecrating America, or his having forsaken books. Not even his allergy to horses bothered me or that he still wasn't divorced. What seemed important was that I was wearing pretty new underwear. The underwire of the bra dug into my ribs every time I took a breath, and I found myself wanting to say, *What exactly is bondage?*

Our conversation was peppered with presumptions. We both said things like *the next time I see you* and *when we get together again*. But at the same time, little red flags went up, highlighting critical areas of incompatibility. Besides observing that we had no interests in common, I found myself assessing him as I would the more empathetic creatures in my domain, as if he were a horse. He was a stallion, of course, and as such, self-centered and domineering. As unappealing as this was, he was the first man to seek me out in years.

Even though I knew we had no future, it was hard not to like someone who said he had wanted to call me for six years. Ten years ago, the men I knew said all kinds of nice things to me. After enough Scotch and sodas, they said they were looking at the prettiest girl in America, and after enough Gallo, I thought they were, too. There were whole evenings filled with boozy platitudes, a whole decade.

And then a decade of neither. No men and no Gallo. A decade of sorting myself out alone, of growing up. Emotionally I had gone through my twenties in my thirties, and now, in my forties, I was beginning to date. It seemed both too soon and too late. But I'd forgotten how nice attention from a man could feel. Maybe my friends were right. I had to give Hank a chance.

Our third date was a picnic dinner at a park overlooking the Hudson River. As we lay on the itchy wool blanket, eating Greek olives, Hank turned to me and said, "I want to marry you."

It felt like a Gallo flashback. As though we were two strangers spinning on bar stools, picking out potential baby names from the wine list. I doubted we'd spent six hours together. He was allergic to everything I loved. He was still married to someone else. I started to laugh and couldn't stop. I didn't know if it was because his question was horrible or wonderful.

Hank started to laugh, too. We rolled onto our backs and laughed up at the sky, big, body-shaking laughs. I laughed so hard tears rolled down my cheeks and into my ears. We laughed and laughed. When we were finished with the big laughter, when it had subsided to an occasional chuckle, Hank rolled back onto his stomach, and I could feel him looking at me.

"I'm serious," he said.

I was still on my back, hooting into the sky. "Just what's *in* those olives?" I stammered.

But I knew that being wanted was the most wonderful feeling in the world.

[12]

*L*AY ME DOWN'S eye worsened steadily all fall. By December, it protruded so much that a large pink mass the size of a golf ball had appeared along the bottom of the eye. It wasn't the tumor, it was the third eyelid being pushed out by the tumor. Because it was December, flies weren't a problem, and Lay Me Down still showed no signs of discomfort. However, it meant the tumor was growing, and even if Lay Me Down seemed otherwise healthy, come spring, flies would be a serious problem.

It was hard for me to look at her bad eye and yet, twice a day, I checked it carefully to make sure she could still blink, to make sure it remained moist. For as long as I could remember I'd been squeamish about medical problems. I assumed it was a result of watching my mother get sick and die. My brother was the same way. Neither one of us went to the doctor for yearly checkups because it made us too nervous. Merely hearing the word *cancer* could give either one of us an anxiety attack. We didn't want to hear about illness and we certainly didn't want to be around it. It was probably a blessing I'd never had children.

But in caring for Lay Me Down, for the first time I felt a shift in the way I handled sickness. I hadn't rushed to euthanize her, and I hadn't hired someone else to do what I couldn't face doing myself, although, so far, there hadn't been much to do. Besides her general care and administering the homeopathic remedies, which might or might not be working, the only thing I'd done was watch for symptoms.

What it actually felt like was a heightened awareness about everything she did. I'd always been able to distinguish between the four horses vocally. I could always tell who was whinnying in the middle of the night and sometimes even why. For instance, if Georgia lost sight of Tempo, her call whinny was long, loud, and quivering with panic as though she was trapped in a burning barn. Tempo's answer was a series of muffled, staccato grunts that sounded like he was underwater.

Hotshot's voice was the most poignant, the most operatic. It started low and ended high, hitting every note in between. He used his whole body to project his distress across the pasture whenever he couldn't see any of the other three.

Lay Me Down wasn't much of a talker but when she did, her whinnies were quick, high-pitched grunts directed at me. Besides greeting Hotshot the first time she met him, I'd never heard her whinny at the other horses or make any sound other than sighing when she was content. My bedroom window faced the pasture so I could hear much of what went on there at night. One of the things I listened for now was any new sound from Lay Me Down or any new vocalization from the other three that might signal something was wrong.

But nothing changed, and Lay Me Down remained openly affectionate. Even Allie, always ready to squelch illusions about what horses were capable of, agreed that Lay Me Down was unusually expressive toward me. It was incredibly flattering. I basked in her devotion, her partiality. She greeted me as soon as I appeared on her horizon. Sometimes I was still in the house when she'd glimpse me through a window and send out her quick little grunts.

If Georgia wasn't vigilant, Lay Me Down would rush to meet me at the pasture gate. When Georgia prevented this by getting to me first, Lay Me Down knew to wait for me in her stall. In the stall she sighed, made eye contact, sniffed my head, my neck, my hands, and let me examine her bad eye without displaying any anxiety. After she finished her grain, I'd pick the ice and mud out of her hooves and then brush her.

Over and over I wondered at Lay Me Down's sweet nature, given her background. It was impossible to understand how she had come through sixteen years of maltreatment with no animosity toward humans. It made her attachment to me feel particularly special, as though in me she sensed a fellow survivor.

My connection to Lay Me Down felt unique in other ways, too. My relationship with her was different from that with any other animal I'd ever had. From the beginning, it felt like it was I who had something to learn from her, I who would ultimately benefit from "saving" her. Her past had surely been as bad as mine but she showed no bitterness, no resentment, no neurotic need to isolate herself from other horses (or people) in order to feel safe. She seemed willing to take big risks—first by being willing to enter the trailer the day I went to the SPCA, and then by attaching herself so strongly to me and then to Hotshot. Her capacity to love seemed enormous. *Where had she learned that? Why couldn't I?*

Lay Me Down had found a sanctuary here and so had I. This small farm was the answer to a thousand prayers, prayers I had uttered to myself during the moments when my childhood seemed unbearable. I'd sit in a locked closet or the basement after being beaten and imagine the place I would live when I grew up. Several details never changed. I imagined a sun-drenched farm with open pasture dotted with grazing Morgans, a big gray barn, several large dogs, and a house with lots of glass. Sometimes the fantasy included a kind and loving husband who shared my passion for horses, but sometimes I saw myself living alone. There would be no yelling or hitting in my fantasy future. I was always the master in my imagined house.

It was nothing less than a miracle to me that my child-hood prayers had been answered, especially after the lost decade of my twenties when it looked like I was throwing my future onto the dung heap. Somehow I'd been able to pull myself out of that self-destructive spiral and, with the move to this farm, had found the first serenity I'd ever known. Lay Me Down and I were survivors, both stumbling onto this farm in the nick of time and both as firmly rooted here now as the umpteenth generation of swallows who flew over a thousand miles each spring to reclaim their barn.

I realized it was a sanctuary I wasn't willing to leave, certainly not for someone like Hank. Maybe it was time to risk a relationship with a man, but Hank wasn't the right one. When Hank said he wanted to marry me on our third date, I was flattered. It didn't matter that we hardly knew each other, that our interests were incompatible. What mattered was being asked. What mattered was that I was wanted. This was the legacy of having been a parentless child; a knee-jerk reaction to male attention. In some ways, that need had controlled my life. All those years of brief, meaningless relationships and the following years of avoiding men completely were opposite sides of the same coin. It was as if I'd thought abstinence could solve an intimacy problem the same way it had solved a drinking problem.

Or maybe abstinence *had* worked. Maybe so many years of not being with a man had allowed me to see something I wouldn't have seen otherwise: that being wanted wasn't enough. This was something I imagined most people learned before they were twenty but I hadn't learned it until a few days before my forty-third birthday.

I was afraid to tell Hank we wouldn't be getting married, we wouldn't be having children. I was afraid to go back to loneliness, but I sensed it was crazy to prolong the relationship. How could I pretend I had a future with a man who was allergic to animals, who couldn't walk into my barn without feeling like all the air was being squeezed out of his lungs? Even if I had been close to loving Hank, I realized I wouldn't give up horses for anyone. But for months friends had told me to give Hank a chance, that we could work around our differences, though they never said exactly how. For months I'd listened to everyone but myself. How could I not? I was the village idiot where men were concerned, the one most likely to fail. So I continued to see Hank and said nothing one way or another about our future.

ONE MORNING, A week before Christmas, I looked at Lay Me Down's eye and knew it was time to do something. The pink mass at the bottom of it seemed bigger, but I knew that the urge to save her, to take some definitive action came from someplace deeper in me. It had to do with the approach of Christmas, the day my family ceased to exist. Mother, father, brother, dog, house—dead or gone, it was all the same to a five-year-old. The Christmases that followed had been spent in other people's houses in which I was alone no matter where I lived, because I was with relatives who didn't want me.

In one house each of my cousins was told to write his or her Christmas wish list on a piece of paper and drop it into a shoe box kept on the coffee table in the living room. I was eight and my list was written in the loopy cursive I'd recently learned in school.

"No, no," my uncle had said when he saw me pushing my folded list through the narrow slot in the top of the box, "we didn't mean you." He was the same uncle whom I'd come upon a week earlier as he was erasing my name and height where I had penciled them on the dining-room doorjamb, adding them to the names and heights of everyone in the family already recorded there.

Later that spring I was sent on, to live with an alcoholic grandfather and his raging wife, in a home where Christmases were boozy days of slurred sentiment, always ending in some kind of violence, as most days ended in that house. Later, I referred to the four years I lived there as my Holocaust years.

What helped sustain me during those four years was my great-grandmother, to whose house, a few blocks away, I frequently ran away. She never knew it, but I was her Lay Me Down, her fugitive from injustice. In her eighties then, Granny Blake intrigued me with her elegance and intelligence, as well as her unconventional lifestyle. She had been born into one of the richest families in Baltimore, but while in her midthirties, following the premature death of her husband, she had relinquished her role as a society matron and begun a career as a journalist. She went on to write five books, one of which was about her ten-month imprisonment in the Lubianka Prison in Moscow on suspicion of espionage, charges that were made while she was a foreign correspondent for the *Baltimore Sun* covering the Bolshevik Revolution (she was fluent in nine languages including Russian).

After her release from prison, she spent several years traveling through Asia, writing about foreign policy and the rise of communism. She returned to America briefly before her spirit of adventure led her to team up with filmmakers Merian C. Cooper (producer of the film *King Kong)* and Ernest Schoedsack in 1924, to make a documentary film called *Grass* about the nomadic Bakhtiari tribe of Persia (now Iran). For a year, the three traveled a thousand miles on foot or horseback with the Kurds of Turkey, filming from Constantinople to the Persian Gulf. The most extraordinary footage began in Basra, where the three filmmakers joined fifty thousand Bakhtiari tribespeople and half a million animals on their twice-yearly migration across six mountain ranges and the Karun River to take their herds to pasture. It was the first film of its kind and featured scenes of my lipsticked great-grandmother, waist deep in a howling snowstorm, scaling the summit of one of the over-four-thousand-foot peaks of the Zagros Mountains.

She spent her later years lecturing around the country,

warning about foreign policies she felt would create something she called third world countries. She also denounced the seeds of hatred being sown by apartheid policies in Africa.

Her house reflected her life as a nomad, with art and artifacts from all over the world gathering dust on her walls and shelves. She'd greet me at the door—a tall, elegant woman, still slender in her eighties, holding one of the Camel cigarettes she chain-smoked in one hand, unaware or unconcerned about the trail of fallen ash that followed her everywhere. "Hello, dearie," she'd say, and I'd follow the high heels and shapely ankles just visible below the hemline of her black silk dress to the living room. We never talked about her son (my grandfather) or his angry wife, but I think she suspected why I so often showed up at her door. Instead, she'd talk about her adventures, especially her months in the Russian prison and the time she'd spent traveling in Africa. Her stories soothed me and helped put my own life into a different perspective. What was a drunken grandfather or an abusive stepgrandmother compared with a cramped cell in a Russian prison or the disenfranchisement of millions in South Africa? She talked about the plight of women and children all over the world, uneducated and impoverished by sexist, patriarchal policies. Even though I was only eight, I knew it was unusual for someone of her class and age to express such sentiments, and I loved her for it. She was the only person in my family who talked about political and social inequities. Perhaps it was there, sitting on her couch and eating butter cookies from a tin while she told her stories, that the seeds of my own desire to write and to work with the marginalized were sown.

Sometimes she'd wrap herself in an enormous musty old fur coat speckled with cigarette burns, and we'd walk a few blocks to the movie theater, where she'd promptly fall asleep and snore through the entire film. Once a week she'd come for dinner at her son's house and invariably singe her hair while lighting a cigarette from one of the candles at the table. I thought she was brilliant so nothing she did embarrassed me, and when I was twenty-one, I honored her by naming my first cat Blake.

I survived my legacy of terrible Christmas memories best by working. Since becoming a social worker, I'd spent every Christmas at my job. My office was on the top floor of an old mansion surrounded by two hundred acres of rolling lawns overlooking the Hudson River. From my window I could watch everything from Windsurfers to oil tankers making their way along the river. Across it, on the distant horizon, were the Catskill Mountains, their high peaks tracing a graceful dark line against the western sky. Behind my desk was a pink marble fireplace and above me was a white vaulted ceiling. It was not the typical office of a social worker. The staff liked to say they worked there for the architecture, and there was no question that the beauty of the place was a perk on days when the tedium of paperwork, voluminous in any social service agency, threatened to drive us into new careers.

The mansion, known as the Manor House, housed twenty adults, all in treatment for alcohol or drug addiction. There was also a stone stable on the property and several other substantial buildings, which at one time had housed the workers on the estate. All these buildings had been converted into treatment facilities for adolescents with substance abuse problems, who resided there for periods of six months to a year.

In the morning I drove through the two stone pillars that marked the entrance to the estate along a narrow winding drive that ended in a manicured, heart-shaped lawn in front of the Manor House. The original owner of the estate had created the lawn as a daily reminder to his wife of his great love for her. For me it had become a reminder of what was missing in my own life. I often wondered what it was like to be loved like that, to be the recipient of such a grand gesture.

The idea that this estate—originally built for the comfort and pleasure of the very rich—was now the home for the desperate and marginalized pleased me. I liked to believe that the original owner would have approved of the new occupants and approved of the humanitarian mission of our agency. Then, one day, the original owner showed up. She burst into tears as she stood on the pecan floor of her former front hall.

"They've ruined it," she sobbed to no one in particular, "*ruined it.*" And she refused to go one step further.

She was rather elderly at the time and so distraught

about the condition and decor of her former home that she
had to be helped from the building and escorted to her car.
A uniformed chauffeur whisked her away. It was easy to
imagine her shock. Perhaps we should have done more to
prepare her for the changes she would see. When she left,
for a moment I, too, felt her enormous loss. It was the way
I had felt as I stood in my grandmother's stable in South
Carolina, surrounded by the decayed finery of her old carriages, missing a world I'd never even known.

Christmas at the Manor House was so depressing for the
patients in treatment that working there left me no time to
ruminate about the trials of my own past Christmases. For
most of those in treatment, holidays and their accompany-
ing stresses represented a time of increased drug or alcohol
use; for many, this was their first experience coping with a
holiday sober. I listened to their stories of previous Christmases spent in soup kitchens, in crack houses, and in jails for
violence, theft, or prostitution. The hardships of my own
past seemed paltry in comparison. Working on Christmas
Day proved as therapeutic for me as it was intended to be
for them.

But this Christmas season something felt different. I
would be there for the residents of the Manor House, of
course, helping them to find the strength to make it through
the holidays. But I also needed to do something more to
help Lay Me Down, something more than wait and watch.
Dr. Grice and I had talked all fall about the possibility of
sending her to the veterinary hospital at Cornell. When to

do it had never been clear. When she couldn't shut the eye? If she seemed uncomfortable? When I asked, Dr. Grice had said I'd know when the time was right. If that was the only criterion, then the time had come.

[13]

WEEK BEFORE Christmas, I finished morning barn chores and went back to the house and called Dr. Grice to ask for a referral to Cornell. An hour later, someone from Cornell called me back to tell me they could admit Lay Me Down the next day, which was a Sunday. I said we'd be there. I began calling around to find someone with a trailer willing to drive us. Allie couldn't because she'd sold her old trailer and hadn't gotten a new one yet. I called her anyway, and she gave me several names to try.

It was hard finding someone to transport a horse six hours one way a week before Christmas, especially to Ithaca, New York, where there was a lot of snow and it was bitter cold. Everyone I called expressed sympathy for my situation, but it was the middle of the afternoon before I found someone willing to do it. His name was Stan, and he lived five minutes away. He told me he was retired from hauling horses but because I was a neighbor and my horse was so ill, he'd be willing to do it. His fee was two hundred dollars, half of anyone else's. His kindness overwhelmed me as well as his compassion for a horse he didn't even know. We'd leave for Ithaca at seven in the morning and he'd bring along his wife, Carol. I'd follow in my own car because I'd be spending the night in Ithaca, after Stan and Carol returned home.

When I hung up, I realized I didn't want to do this alone. Now that I'd committed to going to Cornell, I was filled with anxieties about what would happen to Lay Me Down once she was there. I knew Allie couldn't come with me but I was too upset to think clearly about who could, so I got out my address book and started going through it. As soon as I came to Dorothy's name I reached for the phone. She was the right friend for this trip. She didn't know anything about horses, but she was kind and loving and strong. She was the only friend I had who was from the Midwest, and it showed. She was as sensible as a wool hat.

"Sure," she said without hesitating. "I'll make corn bread."

When we hung up, I couldn't get over the fact that I had a friend who would drop everything for me a week before Christmas to drive someplace as horrible as Ithaca in winter. And who would bring home-baked corn bread, too. Since there was nothing I had to do to get Lay Me Down ready for the trip, I decided to get thank-you gifts for Stan, his wife, and Dorothy.

For Stan and Carol I filled a wicker basket with food from a gourmet shop in Woodstock called Maria's: olive oil, stone ground mustard, chocolate truffles, sun-dried tomato paste, and a dozen of Maria's assorted sugar cookies. Then I bought two thermoses from the hardware store across the street and went back to Maria's to have them filled with ginger carrot soup.

I got a couple of chicken salad sandwiches for Dorothy and me and some rice cakes. For a present, I'd take her to eat at the Moosewood Restaurant in Ithaca and buy her a copy of their latest cookbook.

Later, I packed an overnight bag. We'd be arriving on a Sunday, but Lay Me Down wouldn't see the vet, Dr. Rebhun, until Monday. Even then, they wouldn't be able to tell me whether she was a candidate for surgery or chemo or radiation (or none of them) until they'd completed their tests and analyzed them. But I wanted to stay until Monday on the chance that I might meet Dr. Rebhun. I'd already been warned that this was unlikely, but I felt it was worth a try. In the back of my mind there was another reason for staying, one I was much less willing to admit to myself: I didn't know if I would ever see Lay Me Down again. If Dr. Rebhun determined she was sick enough, he might recommend euthanizing her right there at Cornell. I had no idea what to expect.

I made arrangements for Hannah to do barn chores

while I was gone and to take care of my cat and dog. By nine that night I couldn't think of anything else to do so I put on my parka and went out to the barn.

It was a clear cold night with bright stars and just a sliver of a moon. My footsteps sounded hollow on the snowless, frozen ground, and the arms of my parka swished against my sides as I walked across the pasture. Gray puffs of breath disappeared ahead of me into the darkness. In the distance a cone of white fell from the halogen light over the hayloft doors of my neighbor's barn.

I stopped for a minute to listen for the horses, to see if I could tell where they were—outside foraging or inside eating hay? At this hour, they wouldn't expect to see me. I didn't hear them. I started calling their names as I got closer to the barn so the sound of my footsteps in the pasture wouldn't startle them.

At the barn, I wasn't surprised to see Georgia standing halfway out, studying the night with wild eyes, the only one brave enough to investigate the dark shape moving across the pasture. Her fear touched me, made me want to run my hands along her high round neck to erase the tension and reassure her. I said her name, using my most playful voice, trying to tease her out of her fright.

I could hear Tempo, standing behind her in the aisle, nickering low in his throat the way he did when he was alarmed. I said his name, too, then Hotshot's and Lay Me Down's. I lingered in the entryway, chest to chest with Georgia, her head and neck arched above me while she snorted gray plumes over my shoulder into the frigid air. My arms hugged her sides, my giant horsechild. She had a low tolerance for the cloying demonstrations of affection of which I was occasionally guilty. She preferred a less saturated kind of love: grooming, treats, a good belly or neck scratch. She let me hold her for a few seconds and then shoved me aside to return to the business of eating hay.

Inside the doorway, I felt around on the wall for the raised wooden box built around the light switch to prevent the horses from rubbing against it and turning on the lights or breaking off the switch. I flipped it on, and the barn was filled with a soft yellow illumination, bright enough to make the horses blink sleepy eyes at the sudden glare.

Hotshot and Lay Me Down stood facing each other across the top of Lay Me Down's stall door, their necks crossed like swords, the position horses stood in when they scratched each other's backs with their teeth. But they couldn't exchange back scratches now because Lay Me Down was completely covered by her New Zealand blanket. She also wore a separate neck warmer and an insulated hood with holes for her ears and eyes. She looked like a medieval horse dressed in padded armor ready for jousting.

Even with the lights on, after the others had resumed eating hay, Tempo continued to stare at me with unabated fear. It wasn't enough that he recognized me, he was waiting to see why I was there. It was one of those times I wished horses understood English. *It's OK, Tempo*, I could have told him, *it's just a visit*. I said it anyway, hoping my tone of voice

conveyed the lightheartedness of the situation. To assuage
Tempo's nervousness I had to think the way Tempo thought,
which wasn't always typical of horse thinking in general.
For instance, if I were to approach Tempo while he was
afraid, he'd run away from me. He'd assume I was singling
him out for something nasty, such as a dose of medication or
a visit from the vet. Other horses were soothed by the com-
bination of touch and verbal reassurances, but Tempo
wasn't, not right away. The best way to help Tempo calm
down was to ignore him and give him time to observe me
petting and talking to the others. I would let him come to his
own conclusions about why I was there at such an odd hour.
As I stood nearby, fussing over Lay Me Down and Hotshot,
I could almost see Tempo thinking something like, *Oh, she's
here for that*.

In a few minutes, I disappeared into the tack room and
deliberately made a lot of noise, opening the bucket where
the treats were kept. It was a sound they knew well, along
with the crinkle of the peppermint candy wrappers. When
I came out of the tack room, all three were clumped
together in front of the door, straining their heads forward
into my clenched hand. The fear in Tempo's eyes was gone,
and Hotshot had abandoned Lay Me Down's door. Oh, for
the power of a peppermint. Lay Me Down leaned over her
stall door and stared at us from the eye holes of her hood.
As if I could have forgotten her, the reason for this visit.

I unwrapped the peppermints quickly and handed them
out before anyone—anyone named Georgia—had a chance

to turn this into a competition. When I was done, I held out my empty hands, palms up, and let everyone have a sniff, applying the same principle with treats that I did with Tempo's fear. Show them empty hands and let them draw their own conclusions. It worked pretty well, even with Georgia, who pushed at my hands once, as if to be sure nothing was hidden under my ring, and then turned away.

On my way to Lay Me Down's stall, I gave Tempo a hug, ruffled his mane, and when I was sure he was really his old self, kissed his nose. He only let me do this when he felt secure. Otherwise, it was impossible to get my face that close to his. He'd never completely recovered from being head shy, which was the result of being mishandled during his early years at a public riding stable.

When I pulled the bolt on Lay Me Down's door, she stepped back to give me room to come in. This small courtesy was very different from Georgia's behavior. Georgia didn't seem to realize I was three-dimensional and never allowed me more than a credit card's width of space to maneuver in as I entered her stall.

If Georgia was a bull in a china shop, then Lay Me Down was a geisha at a tea ceremony. Where Lay Me Down was deferential and patient, Georgia was bossy and demanding. Lay Me Down didn't bump me or step on me or push at my pockets even when I knew she smelled a treat. Georgia did all that and worse. Like the time we came home after a long hot ride, and she walked right into the pond with the saddle, bridle, and me still on her, and lay down and rolled. It was so unexpected and so fast that I only just managed to jump off. Saving the saddle was out of the question. I knew other people with Morgans, and they had similar stories. If you looked up Morgans in a breeder's guide, they were described with words like endurance, stamina, and independence. Each one was true. But you could have substituted one word to cover all three qualities: obstinacy. Not that I would have. My Morgan was a Peechums-weechums.

Lay Me Down sighed me into her stall and stared at my hand. I gave her the peppermint and listened to her grind it into powder with her back teeth. I slipped my hand under her blanket to check for shivering and held it against her withers for a few seconds, then slid it down her back until I was resting it on her rump. She turned her head to watch me, exhaling big pepperminty sighs. She was warm and sleek under her blanket, without the thick undercoat the other three horses grew that made man-made coats unnecessary for them.

I walked back toward her head, feeling under the neck warmer as I went and then under her hood, feeling around her ears. She stood still as I checked her, licking her teeth and finding the last bits of peppermint wherever they might have lodged in her mouth. It was impossible to visit her and not come face to face with the pink gelatinous mass quivering along the bottom lid of her eye. I couldn't look at it without feeling queasy, and I wished I had more control over this reaction. But she was beginning to look like a special-effects horse in a horror film.

And always there was the question of pain. The vet said as long as the tumor had someplace to grow—in this case, into the eye cavity, pushing out the eye as it got bigger—there would be pressure but no pain. I didn't think I believed this anymore. My guess was that she was adjusting to whatever pain there was. She wasn't a complainer so we might never know how uncomfortable she really was.

I scratched her neck under her neck warmer, standing on her left side, well out of sight of the bad eye. Now that we were going to Cornell, I didn't feel like I had to check it. I didn't have to be the one to figure out if it was worse today, and if it was time to do something about it. I could just pet her and enjoy how cozy she looked buckled up in her winter blankets.

I wished I could have told her about the next day, told her where we were going and why. Horses experience a lot of anxiety when their routines are changed, and nothing in Lay Me Down's routine included getting in a horse trailer and riding for six hours. Animal communicators claim you can convey reassurance to an animal telepathically. In Lay Me Down's case, I could reassure her by visualizing the journey to Cornell and then visualizing her safe return. I don't think I really believed this, but I tried anyway. It was hard because I didn't know what the vet hospital at Cornell looked like, and I didn't know how long she'd be there or even if she was coming back. Did that mean I was lying when I visualized her return?

Lay Me Down seemed unaffected by my mental efforts

to soothe her, looking perfectly relaxed regardless of what was going on in my head. So often this was the way it was with us. I'd look at her eye and become distressed and then feel better the longer I spent in her calm, unworried presence. Right now she was living in the moment, savoring her peppermint and enjoying having her neck scratched. I tried to do the same.

The next morning I woke up with butterflies in my stomach before I remembered why they were there. Then I rushed out of bed, fed the dog and cat, and went to the barn to do chores and to get Lay Me Down ready for her trip. I took her hood and neck warmer off but left her blanket on for the trailer trip. It was a cold morning, right around zero, and I assumed it would get colder the closer we got to Ithaca. Once we were at Cornell, she'd be in a heated stall so she wouldn't need anything, including her blanket. I wrapped her legs in padded nylon shipping boots that covered her legs from hoof to knee and closed with Velcro straps. They'd protect her legs from bumps and bruises if she was jostled during the trailer ride.

I kept the horses shut in their stalls and piled everything I'd need to bring to Cornell just inside the barn entrance. Hotshot whinnied his objection to being separated from Lay Me Down, and Tempo protested his confinement by pounding his stall door with his front hoof. Georgia bobbed her head over her stall door, trying to nip me every time I walked by. The pile at the entrance included two bales of hay, a fifty-pound bag of feed, a feed bucket with peppermints and alfalfa cubes, her halter, and a lead line. I wanted to keep Lay Me Down on the same diet, including the hay she was used to, in order to lessen the trauma of travel.

At ten minutes to seven, I heard Dorothy's car pull into my driveway, and a few minutes later, Stan's truck and trailer drove slowly toward the barn. I waved him up to the entrance, studying his face through the windshield, recognizing right away that this was a thoroughly decent human being. Carol, too. They were both plump with gray hair and glasses, and appeared to be in their midsixties. They had open, friendly faces, and Carol waved at me before Stan turned off the engine.

Carol stayed in the truck but Stan walked over to introduce himself. His hand felt thick and rough as we shook, and his grip was shy. He'd left his coat in the truck and wore a plaid wool shirt with a white T-shirt underneath, jeans, and work boots. He saw the supplies piled in the barn and suggested we put the hay in the space next to Lay Me Down and everything else in the small storage compartment in the very front of the trailer. I agreed, and we started loading. There was a hay net hanging in the front of the trailer on the side where we'd load Lay Me Down. I got some loose hay from the hayloft and filled it so she'd have something to eat during the trip.

When everything was loaded it was time to get Lay Me Down. I went to her stall and put on her halter. My hands were shaking when I snapped shut her cheek latch. I wasn't sure why I felt so nervous already. Maybe it was the idea that she'd be shut in a trailer for six hours. Or maybe sending her to Cornell signaled the end of whatever crazy hope I had that the growth on her eye would disappear overnight, like a pimple.

She looked so pretty without her neck warmer and hood, so vulnerable, as though I were sending her off to joust without her armor. However, leaving it on in the trailer would have made her too warm. I wasn't even sure she needed the blanket. We'd stop along the way to check her.

I hooked the lead line to her halter, and she followed me out of her stall with stiff, choppy steps. Her lameness was always worse after she'd been confined to her stall for any length of time. She also wasn't used to wearing shipping boots, and I think it must have felt peculiar to have thick pads wrapped around her legs. The other three horses nickered as she passed their stalls, in the early stages of what would soon be full-throated calls of distress as they watched her walk up the ramp and disappear into the trailer.

I led Lay Me Down as far forward in the trailer as we could go, and then I ducked under the padded breast bar that kept her from going any farther, into the small storage space. I clipped a shorter lead line to her halter and snapped the other end to a hook at the front of the trailer. This would allow her enough room to move her head to eat and look around, but not enough to enable her to lie down or walk backward. Stan's trailer had a clear window in the front, which meant Lay Me Down could see the sky above the roof of the truck cab. It wasn't much of a view, but it was better than the trailers that had opaque glass or no window at all.

She seemed relaxed. She was already eating from the hay net hanging in front of her at nose level. I stood right next to the hay net, separated from her by the padded steel breast bar. She looked enormous, filling her side of the trailer with only inches to spare around her. If she hadn't been on a short lead line, she could have reached up and licked the ceiling. It made me claustrophobic so I only stayed long enough to see if she was OK and to check that there was good padding all around her. Just before I left, I hugged her neck and kissed the cheek on the good side of her face. She sighed with a mouthful of hay, misting me with the sweet smell of alfalfa.

Outside, Stan had latched shut the back of the trailer and stood with his hand on the door handle next to the driver's seat, waiting for me to emerge. He'd be making the twelve-hour round-trip in one day so, understandably, he was anxious to get going.

It was difficult to ignore the chorus of frenzied whinnying coming from the barn, but there was nothing I could do about it. Lay Me Down didn't respond, which I took to mean she wasn't distressed to be leaving. When I rode Georgia and we left Tempo and Hotshot behind, running the fence and whinnying after her, Georgia always responded, echoing their fear of separation. Either Lay Me Down didn't mind, trusted it was temporary, or she just wasn't vocalizing her feelings.

We'd agreed that I'd follow Stan because he'd been to Cornell and knew the way. By following I'd also be able to keep an eye on the trailer for the two disasters I feared the most. The first, the trailer and truck coming unhitched, had actually happened to a friend of mine while he was crossing the Throgs Neck Bridge on his way to a horse show on Long Island. He'd looked in the rearview mirror and seen nothing. Fortunately, it was dawn on a Saturday morning, and there was almost no traffic. The other miracle was that the trailer had kept rolling in a straight line and had come to a complete stop all by itself.

The other disaster had never happened to anyone I knew but seemed like something that would occur more often than trailers coming unhitched and that was being rocked over by the horse inside. I'd seen plenty of trailers rock as the horses inside swayed from side to side from boredom or fright, and it hadn't looked like it would take much to tip a trailer right over. Why this had never happened was a mystery and a miracle. By following, I'd be able to tell if Lay Me Down was swaying and I could signal Stan to pull over and stop.

I followed Stan out of my driveway, pausing at the house to pick up Dorothy and the food. When I handed the basket through the truck window to Carol, she laughed in happy surprise. Then she reached out the window and hugged me.

"I knew you were sweet the minute I heard your voice on the phone," she said.

It was the first good feeling I'd had all day.

[14]

HE SIX-HOUR trip went smoothly and at two-thirty Dorothy pointed to a sign with an arrow that read CORNELL UNIVERSITY. We turned and followed Stan up a steep two-mile drive and arrived at what felt like the summit, an alpine village of Ivy League architecture sprawled across an open plateau of blowing snow. He turned into the almost empty parking lot in front of a large stone-block building that looked like an airplane hangar but said EQUINE CLINIC over tall glass-fronted doors. He idled the truck while I pulled into a nearby space and parked.

As soon as I got out of the car I was blasted by a wind so cold it tore my breath away. Four-foot snowdrifts rimmed the parking lot, and the fields around the clinic were rippled in frozen white waves. I ducked my head into the icy needles of wind-driven snow and ran to Stan's truck.

"I'll find out where they want us," I shouted through the window.

He nodded, and I turned and raced across the parking lot toward the front door, wondering how anyone survived four college years of Ithaca winters. The front door was locked and for a second I panicked, thinking we'd come all this way and no one was there. I was shivering as I squinted through the glass doors, gazing down a long, wide corridor. I rapped the back of my ring hand on the glass pane, but the place looked abandoned. There wasn't a human or a horse in sight. Then I noticed a little note posted about waist level near the middle of the door: USE SIDE ENTRANCE.

It didn't say which side, and it felt like I might die of exposure before I figured out how to get inside. I debated whether to go back to the car for my coat but couldn't bear the thought of crossing the windy parking lot twice. Instead, I crept around the edge of the building, trying to stay out of the wind, hoping I'd bump into the right door.

I did. Another sign said RING BELL. I rang and waited. I didn't have much tolerance for cold, and whatever I had was now depleted. I was ready to smash the glass and throw myself against the heat vent I saw in the entryway. Some of my reaction was nerves, but more was genetic. No one in my family liked cold. Movies like *Doctor Zhivago* and *Fargo* fell into the category of Weather Horror Films to me. When I was little and taken to the beach for the first time, I stood in the Atlantic Ocean up to my ankles and wept at the cold. And that was in Palm Beach, Florida, in summer.

No one came, and I pounded at the small red button, feeling frantic. Just when I was ready to give up, a shadow appeared at the far end of the corridor, and as it got closer, it turned into a young woman carrying a ring of keys. She unlocked the door, smiling and apologizing, as I rushed past her into the warmth and quiet.

"How can you stand it?" I blabbered through stiff blue lips.

She smiled again. "Come back in the summer and you'll see."

I shook my head: no, I'd never see. If I lived here, I'd spend July and August dreading December. I'd get cold remembering this cold. I'd move.

Still shivering, "I've brought a horse," I told her. We were standing at one end of a corridor that must have had twenty-foot ceilings. Glass skylights extended the entire length, flooding the building with natural light. The floor was made of beige rubbery tiles with a raised dot pattern designed for good horse traction.

"We've been expecting you," she said. "Lay Me Down?" We introduced ourselves; her name was Eva.

I nodded and followed her for a few feet. Then she turned right into a smaller corridor lined with offices on one side.

"You just need to sign a few things and then you can bring the horse right in," Eva said.

I couldn't quite believe I was doing this—bringing a horse to a veterinary hospital. It was like walking back into my childhood, back to the place where I had learned hopelessness, where I had first connected the smell of floor wax and disinfectant with the feeling of being crushed. Then, just saying the word *hospital* had made me carsick. For me, the connection between a hospital and loss was intractable and vivid. It evoked the day my heart broke. I could not forget.

Yet part of me was excited and hopeful. It was like the first time I dove headfirst into a lake. I was six, standing with ten toes curled over the edge of the dock in a death grip. I arched over the water with my straight arms clamped so tightly against my ears, ready to lead on the way down, that I was deaf to the instructor standing right next to me. I was beyond listening and beyond reason. I was all adrenaline, ready with outstretched fingers and pointed toes to launch myself forward into oblivion. I didn't understand death, but it was all around me and inside me, pressing against me, pulling me down like the cold lake water I was staring at. I would be pretty for death, like my emaciated mother, a vision I would always remember. I dove off that dock in pure terror, understanding it was the bravest thing I'd ever done.

It would always be like that for me; I would have to fling myself off the edge to confront some fear. I had so many fears, so many adrenaline-filled moments, that there were plenty of chances for me to feel brave and daring.

My hand shook as I signed the forms that said I'd pay my bill, I'd allow tests, I was willingly handing over my horse. The office was small and clean. The woman shoving the paperwork across the desk for me to sign was friendly and efficient. The building hummed with heat and electricity. It was safe here, warm and quiet. Still, I couldn't escape my five-year-old horror of anything medical. It was at the center of me, the core memory that structured this experience, thirty-eight years later. I couldn't stop it. I didn't even try. I would survive it. That's what I knew how to do.

So, both fearful and daring, I smiled at the woman. She had come here on a Sunday, a week before Christmas, with the wind howling and the temperature hovering around zero. She was already a hero to me.

"Do you have a horse?" I asked her, tears springing into my eyes. I looked at my lap, hoping she wouldn't notice.

"Yes, I do," she said in a voice that told me she didn't know I was already functioning on overload. But then she reached across the table, touched my sleeve, and said, "And this is where I'd bring him if he ever got sick."

She did know. I rummaged through my bag, pretending to hunt for something. I couldn't bring myself to look at her, to speak. I didn't want to cry in front of a stranger, not even a stranger as nice as she was.

"Now what?" I asked.

"I'll meet you at the front entrance. When the doors open, drive the trailer right inside, all the way in, so I can close the doors behind you. Then we'll unload your horse."

I braced myself to go back out in the cold. She let me out the side door, and the wind flattened my sweater and jeans against my body and sprayed my face again with stinging snow. I pulled my turtleneck up to cover my chin and made a run for Stan's truck. He rolled down his window, and I explained, he nodded, and rolled the window up fast.

Back in my own car, I caught my breath and told Dorothy what we were doing.

"Here's your coat," she said, pulling it out of the back-seat and handing it to me. "The radio just announced that it's ten below zero, not counting the windchill."

"And people pay a fortune to go to this school," I said, burrowing into my parka.

"It's beautiful. I'd go here."

I looked out the window at this campus perched like a religious shrine on a mountaintop. There was a stadium that looked like the Roman Coliseum, a row of greenhouses that belonged to the horticultural school, a building similar to this one called the Bovine Clinic, and a high-rise that could have been a Hilton Hotel but that might have been a dorm. Below us in the distance was a long frozen span of white that must have been Lake Cayuga. It felt like we'd reached the top of the world.

As I was looking around, I glanced in the rearview mirror and saw the large front doors beginning to slide open.

"Time to go," I said.

We ran across the parking lot together, this time entering through the large hydraulically controlled doors that slid open effortlessly along a track in the floor. When they were all the way open, Stan drove the trailer in. Even with the truck and the trailer fully inside, the building felt enormous.

There was easily fifteen feet on either side of the trailer, and the corridor stretched beyond the truck another fifty yards.

The giant doors rolled shut behind us, and it felt like we had entered some sort of biosphere, a world apart from the raging cold outside. Here all was light and warmth and sparkling clean surfaces with a reassuring mechanical hum in the background like the faint rumble in an ocean liner three decks above the engine room. We were dwarfed by the scale of everything. Even the pickup and trailer seemed swallowed up by the expanse of this corridor lined with horse-sized doors labeled SURGERY, RADIOLOGY, INTENSIVE CARE.

I was anxious to get Lay Me Down out of the trailer after her six-hour ride. I also wanted her to know that I was here, someone familiar in this place of strange sounds, smells, and sights. Stan and I lowered the ramp, keeping the kick bar in place until I could unhook her lead and help guide her down. Eva stood at the bottom of the ramp with the others. Lay Me Down backed down the ramp with no fuss and greeted the cluster of people with a misty sigh.

"What a beauty," Eva said, stroking the velvety neck.

I was speechless with pride, as though I had anything to do with creating this remarkable horse, as though she wasn't already a jewel of a being the day she staggered into my life from her muddy paddock at the SPCA. The five of us gathered around her, hands irresistibly drawn to the sweet face, the graceful neck and chest. Lay Me Down lowered her head, the way she did when she was relaxed or sleepy. But her eyes were awake, her brow slightly furrowed as she swept her nose among us at pocket level, politely searching for treats. I got a couple of alfalfa cubes from her treat bucket and broke each one in half so everyone could feed her.

While she ate, I took off her blanket and put it in the trailer to send back with Stan. The clinic felt warm, probably in the midsixties, and she wouldn't be going outside. I unloaded her grain, hay, and treat bucket, stacking everything near a Garden Cart wheelbarrow that was propped against the wall in the corridor.

Stan and Carol were anxious to get going so I hugged them good-bye, and we agreed to stay in touch. Stan had already agreed to return when Lay Me Down was ready to go home. I hardly knew them, yet we were connected by our love of horses and by my gratitude to them.

Eva pushed a button, the big doors slid open, and we watched as the trailer disappeared into the fading afternoon light and whirling snow. They had a long, dark drive ahead of them on icy roads. I looked at my watch and figured if they stopped for dinner, they'd get back to Olivebridge around midnight. I planned to call to make sure they did.

For the time being, we left everything stacked by the Garden Cart, and, with Dorothy on one side and me on the other holding Lay Me Down's lead line, we followed Eva down the long corridor to where Lay Me Down would be stalled. We passed different hospital rooms and two adjoining corridors and finally turned down the last one on the right.

For the first time we walked by large rectangular stalls,

double the size of the stalls in my barn, with black, rubber-mat-covered floors. Most were empty but we saw several healthy-looking horses who nickered at us as we passed. Lay Me Down looked at them but didn't nicker back. It must have felt good to stretch her stiff legs, to be able to walk after being confined in the small trailer for so long, especially to walk on this floor, a wonderful surface for horses that combined the cushiony support of a sneaker with the grip of a snow tire.

Lay Me Down showed no fear of her surroundings. The lead line sagged between us, more a formality than a necessity. She would walk as long as we walked, turn when we turned, and trust that wherever we were going, it was where she wanted to go. Once again I wondered how this kind of trust and gentleness had survived her background. I didn't understand it at all, but it's what made her so special. It's what had opened my heart.

We were nearly at the end of another long corridor when Eva pointed to a stall on the left with Lay Me Down's name on a plastic-coated index card already in a holder on the front of the door. Eva rolled open the door, and Dorothy and I walked in with Lay Me Down. I unclipped her lead, and Eva shut the door behind us.

"I'll bring the wheelbarrow with her things," she offered. "Why don't you stay and visit with her."

When Eva left, Dorothy and I took off our coats and dropped them in a corner of the huge stall. There was a long opaque window at the back, a clear skylight above, and a

193

well-lit view across the corridor to a black Percheron sta-
blemate. At the moment, Lay Me Down was more curious
about her stall than the handsome Percheron across the way,
and she walked around sniffing the floor. It was close to her
dinnertime and I was sure she was hungry. I didn't know if
she was allowed to eat because I didn't know what tests
they'd be giving her tomorrow. I slid open the door and
looked to see if there was a chart or instructions about food.
Sure enough, hanging on a chain outside her stall was a blue
spiral notebook with her name on the front. I opened it and
found a complete medical history forwarded from Dr.
Grice, copies of her sonograms, and the amount and brand
name of the grain she ate, information I had provided over
the phone when they called to confirm that she would be
admitted. Still, there was nothing about whether I could
feed her tonight.

I was impressed at how quickly Dr. Grice had gotten the
medical information to Cornell, and that it was all here,
organized and accurate, before we even arrived. There was
nothing to do but wait for Eva and hope she'd know if Lay
Me Down could have food and water. When I returned to
the stall, Lay Me Down came right up to me, expecting her
dinner. I gave her a hug instead, knowing it was a poor sub-
stitute for a horse who was hungry.

In a few minutes Eva arrived, pushing the cart stacked with
hay and grain, the treat bucket swinging from one of the han-
dles. It would be OK to feed Lay Me Down; none of her tests
required fasting. I followed Eva to the storage room, one stall

away at the end of the corridor, and helped her unload the wheelbarrow. We wrote Lay Me Down's name on labels and put them on her bag of grain, the treat bucket, and the hay. Then I filled a bucket with grain and another with water and walked back with both to Lay Me Down.

Eva said she had things to do and told us we were welcome to stay with Lay Me Down as long as we wanted and to let ourselves out the side door when we were ready to leave. We thanked her for everything and listened to her footsteps fade down the empty corridor until all we could hear was a dull hum coming from the large heat vents placed low along the concrete walls.

While Lay Me Down ate her grain out of a bucket hanging in the corner, Dorothy made a cushion out of her coat and sat on the floor of the stall with her back against the wall. I went to the storage room to get a flake of hay so I could spread it around near where I'd join Dorothy. I bunched up my parka and slid down the wall next to her. And there we were. At Cornell. I felt tiny in the big stall. I felt tiny in the big building. I felt dwarfed by the immensity of Lay Me Down's illness.

I watched my gentle horse eat for a while. With her nose deep in her bucket, her chewing made a nice hollow sound. I couldn't see her bad eye. From where I sat, she was perfect.

"She seems OK," I said. "Not worried or anything."

"She's like Zone, but bigger," Dorothy said.

Zone was Dorothy's black Lab mix, a dog whose sweetness we had run out of ways to describe, who forced us to say things to each other like "Zone's so sweet she'll give you cavities."We called her Zone-Zone the Sugar Cone, or No-Baloney-Zoney-the-Sugar-Coated-Boney, which made no sense but that's what we called her. And Dorothy was right. Lay Me Down was like Zone, but bigger.

"My Lay Me Downie Brownie," I said.

We watched Lay Me Down finish her grain, and then she came over and sniffed her hay. She was right in front of us now, and we could both see her bad eye. No one who walked by and looked at her would wonder why she was there. There it was: wet, pink, gelatinous, the wrong thing to see on a horse's face. It was alarming, too, because it was impossible to look at and not wonder if it hurt.

"Does it bother you?" I asked Dorothy.

She shook her head. "You know those things don't bother me."

True. She'd seen worse. Dorothy was a hospice volunteer. She'd held her boyfriend, Charlie, in her arms when he had died of cancer nine months earlier. The end hadn't been pretty but, in spite of that, Dorothy said being with him when he died was one of the most beautiful experiences she'd ever been through.

Lay Me Down pushed the hay around with her nose, sniffing for her favorite grasses. Maybe she was looking for clover. Horses loved clover. I'd never sat on the floor of her stall like this. My stall floors weren't clean enough, and there was always too much to do when I was in the barn. I would

196

have felt guilty just sitting. However, I didn't feel guilty now, sitting on the spotless rubber floor with Dorothy, watching Lay Me Down eat hay. I felt relaxed and protective of this beautiful animal who blinked at us with drowsy affection.

I looked at my watch. Six o'clock. The snow sounded like sand blowing across the blackened skylights high above us, and shadows filled the corners of Lay Me Down's stall where the overhead lights didn't reach. I hadn't realized it was night already. The outside seemed as remote as the moon, as uninhabitable. If it had been ten below this afternoon, what was the temperature now? At some point we were going to have to leave, make a run across that wind-whipped parking lot for the car. I couldn't bear to think about it.

"Want to look around?" Lay Me Down seemed content and tired. She'd be OK if we left her alone for awhile.

"Sure," said Dorothy, getting to her feet.

We gave Lay Me Down hugs before we let ourselves out of her stall. We visited the Percheron across the aisle, a sleepy black gelding who glanced at us from his hay but didn't come over. I looked at his chart and saw that he was from Connecticut, and he, too, had an eye tumor. It must have been the eye ward and all the horses there, patients of Dr. Rebhun. There were two other horses in this section and sure enough, both had eye tumors, and both charts listed Dr. Rebhun as the vet. Lay Me Down had the only tumor where a mass was visible.

We wandered all over the huge complex, fascinated by the

humanlike services offered, all on a scale for horses. There were operating rooms with two large padded tables, upended and close together like stanchions that the horse stood between to be anesthetized. Once anesthetized, this horse sandwich pivoted until the side of the horse requiring surgery was facing upward on the now horizontal table. This was all done by the push of a button mounted on a wall panel.

We walked through doors marked INTENSIVE CARE and saw a white pony standing in the middle of a stall, supported by a wide sling that passed under her belly and was attached to ropes coming from the ceiling. She was hooked to several IV drips, whose tubes descended from holes in the ceiling. There was no chart outside the stall to tell us what was wrong with her. She looked sound asleep so we kept quiet and tiptoed past.

We passed shower stalls, foaling stalls, stalls for X-rays and MRIs, and stalls with treadmills for stress tests. Everything was immaculate. There wasn't a Q-tip or a roll of Vetrap in sight. There also wasn't a human being, not even Eva, who must have gone home for the night. That we could wander around this expensive facility completely unmonitored amazed us.

We got lost trying to get back to Lay Me Down and wandered up and down the long corridors, passing horses with broken legs, horses with bandaged heads, and horses who looked fine but whose charts described pulmonary problems, blood disorders, and heart disease. We became more interested in finding out where they were from than in what was wrong with them. They were from all over the world: South Africa, Venezuela, Spain, Mexico. Some came from the most expensive breeding farms in America. Others, like Lay Me Down, were beloved backyard pets.

We finally began to understand the building's configuration. It was laid out in the shape of an H, with the addition of two extra lines across the top and the bottom. Lay Me Down's stall was in the bottom right-hand corner of the H. The front door was on the left edge of the middle of the H, the side door on the bottom left. After we'd walked around for an hour, that was our theory anyway.

When we finally found our way back, Lay Me Down had finished her hay and stood, almost asleep, one rear leg bent with her hoof cocked on its toe in typical horse posture of repose. She widened her eyes at us briefly, sighed, and returned to her semi-sleep. I noticed manure in her stall and went to the storage room for a shovel and wheelbarrow to clean it before we left for the night. There was a drain in the middle of the floor for urine and for rinsing down the stalls.

We picked up our coats, said good night to Lay Me Down again, and headed down the corridor for the long walk to the side door.

"Wait a minute," Dorothy said, turning around. "I bet there's a door someplace right near here."

This was Dorothy's little quirk, finding "illegal" doors in places like museums and restaurants, places like the Cornell Vet Hospital. She didn't do it to rebel so much as to gratify

her midwestern sense of logic. If there was a door, use it. A
door marked NO EXIT was just plain silly to her. Clearly it was
an exit, and, what's more, it was also an entrance. We not
only found an unmarked door that opened to the parking
lot, but it didn't lock behind us, so if we could find it again,
it was the way we'd return the next morning.

We drove across a deserted campus and through a nearly
deserted town. Both institutions, Ithaca College and Cornell University, were on semester break; most of the students were gone until mid-January. We checked into our
motel, a nondescript, one-story strip of rooms about ten
minutes from campus, and asked directions to the Moosewood Restaurant. Twenty minutes later, we walked into the
cheerful buzz of a full dining room, eager to taste the food
Mollie Katzen had made famous in the 1977 *Moosewood
Cookbook*.

Whoever was left in town seemed to have congregated
here across steaming bowls of vegetable soup, thick stews,
and garlic mashed potatoes. Sitting in the far corner of the
room was a young man with a guitar singing folk ballads. I
bought both of us copies of their newest cookbook, *Moosewood Restaurant Low-Fat Favorites*, from a stack by the front
door, and while we waited for our pasta, we flipped through
the recipes. It was after eight, and we were both tired from
rising early and the long drive. It felt good to look at the
cookbook, listen to the music, and not have to talk.
Dorothy and I knew each other well enough to know what
we didn't have the energy to talk about that night. For

Dorothy, it was facing her first Christmas without Charlie. For me, it was facing any Christmas, added to which was the anxiety of Lay Me Down's prognosis. For two people on the edge of sadness, we had a pretty good time. The food was delicious, the music reminded us of our youth, and the car was parked right in front of the restaurant.

And that was about as good as that night could possibly get.

[15]

*A*T SEVEN THE next morning, Dorothy and I sat on her bed in the motel room and sipped instant coffee, staring out the window at desolation. It had been too dark the night before to see our surroundings, but this morning we opened the curtains to a view of the motel parking lot, a strip of snowy road and, on the other side of that, the empty parking lot of a CVS. It was a grim landscape in the gray winter light, filled with blowing snow, as though we'd destroyed the planet and all that was left was a howling polar wind and a chain store.

"I wonder what the suicide rate is here," I said.

Dorothy laughed softly. "We just didn't bring the right clothes."

"Expedition gear?"

"Hats."

How could we have forgotten hats? Well, we had, along with long underwear and anything to read. I never went anywhere without a book. Neither did Dorothy. Not that we'd had time to read. There was a television in the room, which was a real treat since neither of us had one at home that had any reception. Ours were used only for watching videos. We thought everything that appeared on the screen was fascinating, even the commercials. We had turned it on the night before as soon as we walked in the room and sat zombie-eyed in front of it until one in the morning. I'd had to drag myself away from a Lean Cuisine commercial with terrific music to call Stan and Carol at midnight to see if they'd gotten home all right. They'd sounded stoned. Then I heard the Lean Cuisine commercial in the background at their house and understood that we were all on the same drug.

Some of the things we had liked about the motel room the night before seemed awful to us in the morning. Top on the list was the television, followed by the view. We decided to check out as soon as we'd packed and spend the rest of the morning at the hospital.

We picked up coffee and corn muffins on the way and got to Cornell around eight, letting ourselves in the same door we had exited from the night before. One glance at Lay Me Down from across the corridor, and I could tell she'd been drugged. She stood swaybacked and droopy from nose to tail. Her eyes were shut, and her head hung almost to her knees. She was utterly still. She opened her eyes briefly when

I slid back her door, but she didn't turn her head to look at me, and she shut them again before I was across the stall. There was clear gel smeared around her bad eye. They'd already run tests.

I checked her water and feed bucket and, for the first time since arriving at Cornell, felt angry. Her grain had been mixed with water and lay untouched in a mushy mess. It meant she hadn't eaten anything that morning. It meant whoever had fed her hadn't read the instructions in her chart. Lay Me Down didn't like her grain wet. It was so simple.

I grabbed the bucket and headed for the garbage can in the storage room. I was so angry I couldn't speak. I couldn't even produce the words to explain to Dorothy. I threw out the wet grain and dried her bucket with a towel. And then suddenly I was sitting on a bale of hay, crying. I couldn't save this horse, not with dry grain or a good winter coat, or by sending her to the best hospital in the world. Not even by loving her.

I couldn't save myself either, from feeling five years old again, helpless, and horrified. I knew that my rage and deep sorrow was thirty-eight years old, preserved perfectly intact, like a buried artifact suddenly exposed to the light. My past was more real than ever, more acutely alive in me than ever before. It had taken my love for this sick horse to make me willing to finally face death after all these years, to cry for the first time about the death of my mother and the loss of my family. It had taken me thirty-eight years to not drink or joke or lie about how awful the rest of my childhood had been. It was hard to accept that it was mine. All these years I had coped by distancing myself from it, as if it had happened to someone else, a child in a story.

I sat on the bale of hay and sobbed. A memory surfaced, a memory of a day soon after my mother's death, when I had just gone to live with my grandmother. "Where's my mother?" I'd asked her.

"You're not to talk about her anymore," she'd answered, a bejeweled finger shaking in my face. My mother was a forbidden subject; I'd been bad to bring it up. Years later, one night at the dinner table, just after I'd gone to live with my grandfather, I asked him to tell me about my mother, who was his daughter. Before he could answer, he started to cry.

"Now see what you've done," his wife hissed at me and I was sent to my room.

Dorothy walked into the storage room and sat next to me on the bale of hay. I couldn't look up, but I felt her hand making circles on my back.

"What is it?" she asked.

I didn't know what to say, how to explain the depth of my grief. It seemed so private to me, something I could only talk about with my brother, the other person who had gone through it. I didn't know how anyone else could understand the shame connected to what we had experienced. There was no rational basis for this shame but it was there, bigger than our sadness. It was the shame of being unwanted, unloved. So I had yearned for the day I would belong only to myself, free from anyone who could make me feel like a burden, who could leave me or die, as if that was possible.

"They screwed up her feed," I said, looking around for a paper towel.

Dorothy pulled a clean tissue out of her pocket and handed it to me. I blew my nose and took a deep breath. "Is it awful without Charlie?"

She shook her head. "Not anymore, but I cried a lot at first."

I hardly ever cried. That's probably why I was crying now, because of all the things I had never cried about before. It was as though Lay Me Down and my childhood had merged into the same thing: losing what mattered, losing love. In a crazy way, it felt like Lay Me Down had been taking care of me ever since I got her, bringing to life parts of me that had died with my mother. By her gentle affection I felt restored to the status of someone who mattered, someone who was needed. She gave me that, a sense of family. We both had belonged to nobody, nobody who cared, and now so late in our lives, this miracle had occurred. We had come together on my farm, and for the first time, we had both been free from our fears.

Voices came from the corridor. It sounded like a crowd. I got up and splashed water on my face from the faucet at the utility sink. I left the empty bucket beside her grain. There was no point feeding her until the sedative had worn

off. I took a leaf of hay to put in her stall so she'd have something sweet to smell as well as something to nibble when
she started to come around.

Outside the storage room the corridor was filled with
young women. We counted ten students and one older
woman, the vet teaching the class. One of them told us
they were in their final year of vet school. I asked where the
men were. She said there were no men in this class, that
more than seventy-five percent of the vet students were
female. We stood back and listened while the teacher
presented Lay Me Down's case. Then they all trooped into
her stall to examine the patient.

It was a funny scene, this group of young women gathered around my sleepy horse. It reminded me of an early
riding class years ago: a cluster of seven-year-olds pressed
close to a tall horse, faces tilted upward toward the graceful neck and the great round eyes, thrilled if the eyes looked
their way, singled one of them out. Lay Me Down's stall
echoed with the sound of those little girls. They gathered
around her, their voices full of tender concern, though
now they were in their late or midtwenties and draped with
stethoscopes instead of braids.

Dorothy and I watched from across the corridor, well
out of the way of the class studying eye tumors. No one had
asked who we were. I didn't know if they realized I was the
owner of the horse who stood quietly under their scrutiny.
The class seemed informal, perhaps a follow-up to whatever test had been done earlier that morning. Some of

them listened to her heart and lungs with their stethoscopes. Some just stroked her neck, murmuring encour-
agement at the sleepy face. I loved watching them discover
her. "What a sweetie," they said. "What a wonderful horse."

They didn't stay in her stall long, ten minutes at most,
and then they filed out, disappearing down the corridor as
they went on to the next case. Lay Me Down stood immo-
bile in the middle of her stall, still heavily sedated. Her
lower lip hung open, exposing her bottom teeth. Her eyes
were slits of dark moisture under gooey lids. I brought in
the leaf of hay and scattered it around right under her
nose. I got a label from the storage room and wrote a
reminder about not wetting down her feed and stuck it on
the front of her chart.

I didn't know what else I could do. It might be hours
before the sedative wore off and she was in any shape for a
visit. I had been warned that meeting Dr. Rebhun was
unlikely. I had to work the next day and so did Dorothy. There
was nothing to do but go home and wait for a phone call.

This time we left by the designated door, stopping to tell
Eva about Lay Me Down's grain. She apologized and said
she'd tell the girl who fed Lay Me Down herself.

Dorothy and I were quiet as we drove through the snowy
landscape of dairy farms and hay fields scattered across
open hills, stretching all the way to the horizon. Huge silos
rose into the gray sky, some bearing a farm name in large
letters across the top: Tillson, Kingsley, Hardwick. The
highway wound before us, a dark path through the broad

white valley, almost empty except for the occasional car going in the other direction. I could feel the wind, like an invisible hand tugging at the steering wheel. Dorothy leaned against the headrest, looking straight ahead, *Moosewood's Low-Fat Favorites* unopened in her lap.

It was three days before Christmas and I was thinking about death and dating. I was thinking I had no future with a man who was allergic to horses.

"Tell me again why it isn't insane for me to be dating someone like Hank," I said, glancing at Dorothy. As I turned my head, I felt a small shock in my lower back, like the snap of a rubber band. It was a feeling I knew well. "My back just went," I said through clenched teeth. In another few seconds I could only hold myself upright with my arms, one hand pressed into my seat, the other gripping the top of the steering wheel. With every bump in the road, a sickening pain shot through my lower back and down my legs. Lifting my right foot from the accelerator to move it to the brake was excruciating as I eased the car onto the shoulder of the highway and stopped.

"Just tell me what to do," Dorothy said. She was familiar with my back episodes and knew how debilitating they could be.

"I need to lie down," I said, beginning to panic. I couldn't imagine how I would get myself into the backseat, even with Dorothy's help. A gust of wind rocked the car, triggering spasms of pain that made me nauseous. Sitting upright was unbearable. Dorothy got out of the car and began moving our luggage so she could lower the backseat. I had to wait until she was finished before I could recline the driver's seat as far as it would go, which wasn't flat, but provided some relief.

I needed ibuprofen. "Four," I told Dorothy. "They're in my purse." I swallowed the pills without water and asked Dorothy to pack the plastic bag from yesterday's sandwiches with snow from the side of the road. I'd ice my back and wait twenty minutes for the ibuprofen to kick in and then, maybe, with Dorothy's help, I'd be able to make it into the backseat.

We kept the car running with the heat on high, but I shivered anyway. It was all nerves. I was terrified to be that helpless, in the middle of nowhere. I glanced at the gas gauge, imagining a worse disaster. If we ran out of gas, we might freeze to death. The gauge showed three-quarters full. We were about two hours out of Ithaca with another four hours ahead of us. It seemed impossible that we'd ever make it home. But in the state I was in, it seemed that nothing good could happen. I was shivering so hard my teeth chattered.

Dorothy was the picture of calm, one hand resting on my arm while the other fished through my purse looking for my cell phone. "We'll call your chiropractor to see if she can meet us at the office."

I nodded my head. "Good idea."

She pulled out my cell phone and flipped it open. There was no reception. Zero. We would die in a dead zone, one of life's little ironies. My brain careened through a list of people I'd heard of who'd frozen to death: Shackleton, Mallory, Doctor Zhivago—almost. Maybe we'd be asphyxiated first. I opened the window a crack, and a blast of frigid air swept across my face.

"There's a police car behind us," Dorothy announced.

"He'll think I'm stoned," I mumbled. Still, I was relieved. Maybe he'd help Dorothy get me into the backseat.

A face appeared at the driver's window wearing wraparound sunglasses and one of those tan wide-brimmed state-trooper hats.

"What's the problem?" he asked, opening my door and bending down to peer into the car. The car filled with cold air as the wind blew the door hard against his back. He reached behind him to hold it open with one hand while removing his sunglasses with the other. His eyes scanned the interior of the car before coming to a rest on mine. His face was pale and chubby; he couldn't have been more than thirty.

I explained about my back. "I just need to lie flat."

"Sure you don't want an ambulance?" he asked.

God, did I look that bad? "No, no," I assured him, "if you could just help move me."

"We're not supposed to do anything medical, ma'am," he said, sounding doubtful.

"It's not really medical," I pleaded, "it's more in the category of helping an old lady cross the street."

He smiled at my stab at humor and seemed to consider the options. He looked up and down the highway.

"We need to get you off the road," he said. "This is a bad place to stop."

"My friend can drive," I told him, "*if we can just get me out of the way.*"

Maybe he could tell I was the kind of person who wouldn't sue even if he dropped me on my head, or maybe he just wanted to hurry us off a dangerous spot on the highway. Whatever it was, he finally agreed to help move me.

He opened the hatchback first so when they got me that far, they could just slide me in like a two-by-four. Then, as gently as he could, he pulled me out of my seat into a standing position. I teetered between him and Dorothy with my arms around their shoulders, letting them support all my weight so there would be no compression whatsoever of my spine. The pain was horrible anyway, as though someone were cutting me in half with dull scissors. Every time my back did this, I wondered if I'd ever be able to walk again. It seemed impossible that such pain wouldn't cause permanent damage.

They lowered the top half of me into the car, letting my knees bend so my feet were still on the road. Then the trooper opened the back door and knelt inside, pulling me the rest of the way into the car by my armpits. Flat on my back, if I didn't budge an inch, I was pain free. At the moment, it seemed like a miracle.

"Thank you," I said, releasing a long sigh. Dorothy handed me the plastic bag with the snow and packed various things around me to prevent me from rolling. We thanked the trooper again and then we were on our way.

With every bump and jolt of the car, the pain returned, but I was so relieved to be moving in the direction of help, it no longer panicked me. When we got closer to home, we'd call my chiropractor again. I thought about Lay Me Down and how glad I was that this hadn't happened before we'd gotten her to Cornell. However bad this felt, Lay Me Down's problems were far worse, and I was grateful I'd been able to accompany her to the hospital.

On Christmas morning I woke up after an uncomfortable night's sleep, knowing that I didn't have to do anything. There was no way I could. There would be no barn chores, no counseling clients through the Christmas blues, no putting in an appearance at my neighbor's annual Christmas party, and no meeting Hank and his daughter for Christmas dinner across the river. Hannah would take care of my horses, and, at noon, some angel from a home-help agency was coming to give me a bath. Aside from the possibility of a late-afternoon visit by one or two friends, that would be the highlight of the day. Maybe the home-health aide would even change my sheets!

My world had shrunk to the size of my king-sized bed, which was piled with books, magazines, and videos I had to hold in my teeth as I crawled on my hands and knees to insert them in the VCR across the room. Next to me, spilling off the bedside table onto the floor, were water bottles, open boxes of crackers and rice cakes, a box of clementines, vitamins, a big bottle of ibuprofen, a couple of empty soup bowls, and a half-eaten box of Whitman's chocolates. Every time I crawled to the bathroom I had to navigate through the clutter to get there.

As long as I didn't move in certain ways, my pain was no longer excruciating. Though I was still unable to sit up or walk, I recognized subtle signs of progress. Things didn't seem too bad.

A few hours later, I was lying back with my eyes shut, luxuriating in the warmth of a lavender-scented bath. Kneeling on the floor next to me was the home-health aide, a middle-aged woman with graying hair who'd brought along her knitting and a photograph of an orange kitten she'd gotten herself for Christmas. She had a southern accent and told me she'd been born in a log cabin in Missouri.

"I'm the oldest of eleven. I've been taking care of someone my whole life," she said.

Did she mind? I couldn't tell. She seemed easygoing, the kind of woman who never complained about anything.

"But I'm not here to talk about me," she said. "Tell me how you're doin', honey?"

I opened my eyes and turned to look at her. Her glasses had slid to the middle of her nose and I could see how twinkly and blue her eyes still were. "I feel pretty good." I smiled at the kind face. "I've managed to get out of Christmas."

A funny little laugh escaped from her throat and she bent over slightly, feeling for the cameo pinned at the neck of her blouse, as though checking to see if she was still properly covered. "Me, too!" She rocked on her heels, trying to contain her laughter. "Don't you just *hate* Christmas!"

After my bath, she changed my sheets and then sat in a chair knitting while we watched a video. As we said our good-byes later that afternoon, we agreed that, without question, it was the best Christmas we'd ever had.

[16]

$\mathcal{A}$ WEEK LATER I was up and walking but not ready for the twelve-hour round-trip car ride to bring Lay Me Down home, so Stan and Carol agreed to get her without me. The day they left, I spent forty-five minutes on the phone with Dr. Rebhun, who described the tests, the results, and the options. The tumor was large, invasive, and inoperable. Because of its location in her brain, it had been inoperable from the day it had formed. Horses bled to death on the operating table when they tried to remove tumors that near the eye. For Lay Me Down, the only "options" were when to euthanize her, now or later.

"You'll know when the time is right," Dr. Rebhun said.

"How?" I gripped the phone with both hands. "How

will I know?" What I really meant was, *I don't trust myself to know*.

Dr. Rebhun was quiet for a long moment. Then he said, "If I knew, I'd tell you."

His voice was kind, apologetic. We were no longer talking about medicine. On the subject of euthanizing, my judgment was as good as his. That's what he was telling me. He couldn't save her and he couldn't tell me when to kill her. She was out of his reach.

When Lay Me Down returned from Cornell, I called Dr. Grice. I asked her how I would know when it was time to euthanize Lay Me Down, but what I was hoping was that she'd make the decision. She didn't. Her answer was just as vague as Dr. Rebhun's.

"It wouldn't be wrong if you did it now, and it wouldn't be wrong if you didn't," she said.

I was sitting at the kitchen counter, looking out the window while I was talking to her on the phone. The horses were eating the morning hay I'd scattered on top of the snow in the pasture. Lay Me Down was wearing her blue coat and standing next to Hotshot. Georgia and Tempo were together, several yards away. All four of them were in the sun. The thermometer on the tree near the window read thirty.

Suddenly I knew what I wanted, what I wished for Lay Me Down before she died. A spring day full of the smell of moist earth and sweet new grass when she could stand in the sun without her coat. If I was to play God, I wanted to give her a sunbath. It meant keeping her alive for four more months, until April. I had no idea if that was possible, but it was my goal. I told Dr. Grice.

"Yes," she said, "horses love the sun."

I didn't really know what facing death meant. I knew more about avoiding it, about drinking and sleeping around to blot out the memory of death and, later, about choosing loneliness over the possibility of facing more grief. Being with Hank was more of the same, a relationship with a built-in ending. If you didn't care much, there was nothing much to lose. It was a lifestyle.

It was a lifestyle I'd had to relinquish because of a sick horse. Cornell was our last hope and now that that hope was gone, there I was, facing the thing I'd tried to avoid all my life. Loss. This one felt as big to me as losing a dear friend, a relative, anyone I'd ever loved deeply and unconditionally. Maybe loving a horse was like that because they were big, or because you expected them to live so long. Maybe because having a horse meant your life had been touched by a beautiful mystery.

After Cornell, Lay Me Down was different. She moved to the edge of the herd and dozed standing up while the others ate hay. She didn't sigh as much and her eye contact was less sustained. Before Cornell there had been an exuberant quality to her affection, an intensity. She used to lock me in her gaze as soon as I appeared on the horizon, and I'd feel pulled toward her by that stare. Now when she saw me, she looked briefly, then looked away. That was normal for horses but not for Lay Me Down.

At first I thought her distance was because she was recovering from her ordeal, her journey and everything she'd been through. But weeks later she still seemed aloof.

"I think she's depressed," I told Allie in my barn one January night as I turned on the light.

We watched Lay Me Down's breath billow over her hay in long white puffs. Hotshot stood outside her stall door, blinking at the sudden illumination. Georgia and Tempo were eating hay across the aisle in Tempo's stall. Lay Me Down was royal blue from head to tail, dressed in her full winter gear: hood, neck cover, and blanket. I slipped my hand under her blanket and checked along her side for shivering. She felt warm and fuzzy.

For once Allie didn't accuse me of anthropomorphizing. "Could be the anesthesia," she said. "Sometimes it takes months for the effects to wear off."

Lay Me Down had greeted our unexpected night visit in her new, more casual way: a glance, a faint sigh, and then she went right back to eating hay. I missed the way she used to be, her engaging stare, the big wet sighs misting some lucky recipient, usually me. Everything I wore was covered in horse snot or sticky from peppermints. Even my car was never without the wide gray lick marks swirled across the windows. And recently, Lay Me Down's teeth had left a jagged white trail across the smooth red hood. I couldn't feel angry even though I tried. A horse shouldn't be allowed to eat your car. I'd said no and pushed her away, but there was no threat in my voice, nothing that would frighten her.

It would have been different with Georgia. With Georgia I would have rushed at her in a fury of waving arms and loud nos, and she would have flicked her tail at me and trotted, stiff-legged, to a safe distance to wait until I had returned to my senses. No matter what she had done, it was never Georgia's fault. *I* was the crazy one who periodically exploded for no good reason. Morgans are without contrition, the *Who, me?* of horse breeds.

Lay Me Down had enough contrition for both of them. Maybe too much, like people who apologized when someone else stepped on them.

"Maybe she knows she's dying," I said. I felt funny saying this out loud in front of Lay Me Down. You never know.

Allie shook her head. "She's not dying."

For a second I felt elated. Dr. Rebhun was wrong. My smart friend was about to tell me what we could do to get rid of this tumor. "She's not?"

"Not for a while."

My elation vanished. My smart friend was being literal. Lay Me Down was eating hay, not dying. What would dying look like?

"Think she can make it to April?" I asked.

Allie looked at her bad eye. "I don't know," she said.

No one I asked could tell me when to euthanize Lay Me Down. I called Dr. Grice back and made arrangements for her to come twice a month. Dr. Grice would measure the growth of the tumor, check Lay Me Down's vital signs, and give me medicated drops to help keep the eye moist and clean. Then I hung up and called Clayton Barringer. He had a backhoe and dug graves for the town cemetery. He also dug horse graves. I wanted to bury Lay Me Down on my property but didn't know if a hole could be dug when the ground was frozen. Should he dig it now, before the frost line got deeper?

"Frozen ground's no problem," he said, air whistling between missing teeth. "Call me the day before. That way it'll be ready and the vet can do it right by the hole. Is the horse strong enough to walk to where you want the hole dug?"

Something I'd never thought of, how to get Lay Me Down from where she died to where she was going to be buried. This was part of not facing death, having no plan for the obvious. I'd never thought about this, but it made sense. Bring the horse to the hole and euthanize her there. Creepy but practical. It was better than whatever the alternative was. Dragging? Part of knowing when to euthanize her meant not letting her get so weak she couldn't walk. But what if it happened suddenly? What if she was normal one day and the next day couldn't get up?

"I don't know," I said. I resisted the urge to apologize, to cry, to ask him to come over and shoot her between the eyes right then and take her away so all signs of her were gone by evening chores. I resisted the urge to explain why I didn't know if she'd be able to walk to her own grave or not. It didn't matter.

I heard him light a cigarette and blow out the smoke.

"Don't you worry," he said after a long pause, "I'll arrange him in the hole real pretty."

I resisted the urge to say *her*.

Facing death meant getting up every cold dark morning and walking to the barn and doing exactly what I always did. It meant going to work and coming home and going back to the barn to do evening chores. It meant sticking to the routine. Was I the only one who didn't know that facing death meant facing life? They were exactly the same. Even Georgia seemed to know this. It must have been obvious to her that Lay Me Down was sick, but it made no difference. She still hated her. She still chased her away whenever she got the chance.

Hotshot stuck to his routine, too. The ugly pink growth, now the size of a tennis ball, didn't change his ardor. When she came back from Cornell he was the only one I allowed out to greet her, the only one of the three who would give her the wholehearted welcome I wanted her to have. And he did. He sniffed and nickered the length of her until she grew annoyed and flicked him away with her tail. Already I was sad, thinking how he would miss her. I got a taste of it when she was at Cornell, watching him look for her up and down the fence line several times a day. He'd stand at the gate and whinny in the direction of the pasture where he'd first seen her. There was something almost unbearably sweet in his thinking she might be there, just across the pond where he couldn't see her. What must he think of me? That I would separate him from her for no reason?

At the beginning of February I got around to making some New Year's resolutions. It was a short list, only one item: end the relationship with Hank. My resolution was connected to Lay Me Down. Life is short, do what matters. My horse was dying and sadness made me bold, woke me up, gave everything an edge, a now-or-never quality. Lay Me Down was my muse, my inspiration to find meaning in loss, to make peace with it, to find the beauty in it. If nothing else, to see the truth of it.

A few weeks earlier Hank had given me an ultimatum. Either we lived together or he'd end our relationship. He wanted me to move there, into the house he had shared with his wife, with his Hudson River School paintings, his brown linoleum kitchen floor, and his blue Mexican water glasses with the air bubbles. I felt as if he was asking me to slip into someone else's old dress. I never seriously entertained the idea, but I had put off telling him because that was what I did. I avoided endings. Besides, I didn't take his threat seriously. This was a man who had waited six years to call me. It was important to take my time, chose the right moment. This was someone's heart. Then something right out of a movie happened.

"Sorry about you and Hank," a woman we both knew said to me in the grocery store. "I didn't think he was the kind of man to go for someone that young."

It was as though she'd punched me. I gripped my cart, hoping she didn't realize it was holding me up. "What?"

Her hand flew to her mouth. "You didn't know?"

I was filled with such loathing for this woman I could have struck her, reached over and slapped that shocked look right off her pretty face. For a second, hating her took my mind completely off what she had said. I didn't trust myself to speak. If I opened my mouth flames would engulf her. I'd incinerate the whole store.

When my knees stopped shaking, I turned and walked out, leaving the cart half full of groceries and the woman standing there with her hand still covering her mouth. I drove toward Allie's house in a bubble of numb rage. I kept seeing the face of the woman in the grocery store—the wide eyes, the open mouth hidden behind the slender hand. No suffering I could imagine was enough to punish her for what she had done. For a few minutes hating and blaming her worked to keep my mind off what she had told me, but halfway to Allie's I forgot about her and switched to hating Hank. By the time I was there, I hated all men, and before I was out of the car, I hated all men and all women. I was in no shape to talk. I felt possessed, as though I could have spun my head three hundred and sixty degrees and vomited frogs. Before Allie saw my car, I turned around and left.

It was four o'clock and already getting dark. When I reached home I walked from room to room, flipping on lights. I couldn't stop moving. No matter where I went, I saw her face, the look of astonishment, her beautiful hand—slender with smooth white skin. She hardly knew me and she had brought me this news of Hank's betrayal.

I was obsessed with her, frozen in the moment of what she must have intended as a condolence, as words of solidarity.

I changed into barn clothes: long underwear full of holes, sweatpants, turtleneck, sweatshirt. Everything smelled of horses. Downstairs, I took the insulated snow pants off the hook on the stairwell wall. They smelled like the barn, too. Sometimes I worried that my whole house smelled like the barn.

I grabbed a bag of carrots out of the refrigerator and slipped my boots on by the dining-room door. The snow squeaked as I crossed the lawn and ducked under the fence into the pasture. The horses were there waiting, all four of them, right by the fence. They jostled each other, pressed around me, blowing columns of frozen breath. This was when Georgia could be her most possessive, her most obnoxious. Still, I loved this moment, seeing them again after a day apart, smelling them. I said their names, teased them by crinkling the bag of carrots. I gave them each one, then hurried them along to the barn before Georgia could spoil this moment with her jealousy.

Georgia followed me into the barn, bumping up against me when I stopped to turn on the lights. She amazed me. If she was a person I'd hate her. She was the woman behind you in line at the grocery store who bumps you with her cart, who slaps her checkbook onto the little transaction platform while you're still waiting for change, who casually mentions that your boyfriend is cheating on you.

Georgia flattened her ears and stood in the entry, keep-

ing everyone else out. Charming. Tempo ignored her and
shoved her aside. He was the only one who could get away
with this, who even dared try. Hotshot and Lay Me Down
paced around outside. I could hear the crunch of snow as
they circled. I didn't trust Georgia to behave herself waiting for dinner. I got her to follow me to her stall by crinkling the bag of carrots. Once there, I gave her one, then
left, shutting her in.

Right away Hotshot and Lay Me Down knew it was safe
to come inside. Lay Me Down hurried to her stall with
quick, stiff steps and heaved a big sigh as soon as she was
there. She stretched her neck toward the ceiling and curled
back her upper lip until it was almost touching her nostrils,
and gave herself a deep whiff of her stall. It was a gesture
of utter contentment. I understood. It was the way I felt
about home, too.

Hotshot stood just outside her stall in the aisle, her
guardian, her devotee. I couldn't look at him without an
ache in my chest. I kept seeing him trot up and down the
fence when she was at Cornell, the innocence of his distress, how distressed he would be again.

Tempo went into his own stall and pawed at the wall
with his front foot. BAM! BAM! BAM! It was so unlike
his general attitude, this display of adolescent impatience,
this boldness. But it was his unfailing routine, every morning and every night. Like Lay Me Down sniffing her stall, I
thought kicking the wall was Tempo's way of expressing
joy at being home. Or maybe it was the way a predominantly

anxious personality could say to the world, *You might think I'm a scaredy-cat but I'm really a big, tough guy*. BAM! BAM! BAM!

I scooped different amounts of grain into four buckets, added medication, vitamins, and supplements and broke up the carrots and added those. I brought Tempo's out first to get him to stop kicking the wall and because he took the longest to eat. Then Lay Me Down's, because she got so excited when she saw Tempo's bucket that she'd pace around her stall, and I couldn't stand to make her wait. Then Hotshot's, for no reason except to get him out of the aisle, and finally Georgia's, whose head arched and bobbed over the stall door, indignant at being last. I apologized, told her she was gorgeous, she was wonderful, the best horse in the whole world. Her ears flattened, and she shoved hard at my shoulder with her nose, almost spilling the contents of the bucket as I hooked it to the ring in the wall. Fat chance she'd fall for flattery. I'd made her wait!

I climbed the steep spiral stairs to the hayloft where there were six hundred bales, give or take, stacked all the way to the roof. There was a narrow path winding through the bales so I could drop hay through holes in the floor to the stalls below. Georgia was the only one who'd move out of the way when I dropped the hay. I'd warn her and she'd move. The others didn't get it. They'd look up at me through the hole and get hay dropped on their heads. I tried to do it while they were still eating grain so I wouldn't have to spend twenty minutes brushing hay out of forelocks and manes. I didn't know why Georgia understood and the others didn't. You'd think she would have explained it to them.

After I dropped the hay, I opened the wide hayloft doors that overlooked the pasture, my neighbor's hay fields, and, twenty miles away, the ridge line of the Shawangunk Mountains. I sat in the doorway, dangling my legs over the edge. It was clear and cold and, in a few hours, the sky would be filled with stars. Right now it was a blue-black with a silver glow still visible to the west. To the left, on the other side of the pasture fence, yellow light spilled out of the tall back windows of my house, across the deck and onto the snow. I could see almost the entire downstairs: my grandmother's red tapestry, the red couch, red dining-room chairs, a red colander hanging from a beam in the kitchen.

Hank liked blue.

It was so quiet I could hear ice crystals blowing across the surface of the snow. I listened for a long time, smelling the hay around me, watching the stars emerge one by one in the blackening sky. I cried because it was a terrible way to end a relationship. I cried because I was afraid it was too late for me to find love. I cried because I was losing Lay Me Down.

But I didn't cry for Hank.

[17]

PRIL 25TH WAS unseasonably warm. At seven in the morning the thermometer on the porch off my bedroom read sixty-eight degrees. I knelt at the head of my bed and looked out the window into the pasture. Lay Me Down was lying by herself in the sun near the fence. Her head was up, and her front legs were bent at the knee, tucked under her chest. The other three horses were standing in the sun at the entrance to the barn. I opened the window and called Lay Me Down's name. She raised her head and looked at me. She wasn't wearing a coat, and in the sun she was a glossy mink brown.

I grabbed my cell phone and headed for the pasture barefoot, still in my pink plaid pajamas. The grass was prickly and wet, the ground cold in spite of the warm

morning. I ran on tiptoes across the lawn and ducked under
the fence near Lay Me Down. She watched as I approached
but didn't get up. The other three watched from the barn
but didn't come over. None of this felt right, not Lay Me
Down here alone and not the other three standing so far
away. Why wasn't Hotshot with her?

I knelt in the grass in front of her and stroked her neck,
her cheek, her nose. I said her name, asked her what was
wrong, why she was lying alone so far away from Hotshot.
I looked at the tumor, still about the size of a tennis ball, but
who knew what it was doing inside. She was warm where
the sun fell on her. I ran my hand all the way down her
spine, down the silky smooth contours of the muscles
along her back. She turned her head to watch me, only her
good eye visible from where I crouched near her shoulder.
I held her gaze a long time. I wanted to remember her face,
the grace of her body outlined in the early sun.

I called Dr. Grice and left a message with her answering
service. I said, "Today's the day. Could she come this afternoon?" The answering-service woman said, "Today's what
day?" I told her Dr. Grice would know.

I hung up and went back to the house for a camera. I was
afraid I wouldn't remember Lay Me Down exactly the way
she was, right then, so beautiful lying in the grass. I wanted
to keep her with me, to keep this morning close to me for
as long as I lived. I thought a photograph could do that,
something to hold in my hand.

I took several pictures. She didn't move and neither did the other three still standing by the barn, watching. It was extraordinary to me how all of them knew, how I knew, too. Lay Me Down had crossed some invisible line and had already begun to separate from us.

I went back to the house to change. There was a message on my answering machine from Dr. Grice. She'd be at my home at two. I called Allie and asked her to come. She said she'd arrive by one o'clock. Then I called Clayton Barringer. He had wanted a day's notice, but I asked if he could come that morning to dig the hole, right away. He said it would take him an hour to drive the backhoe.

I went back to the barn to feed the horses and do morning chores. I didn't know what to do about Lay Me Down. Should I bring grain out to her or leave her alone? I led the other three inside and shut them in their stalls while they ate. I threw a bale of hay out the hayloft doors and went outside to separate it into four sections, one for each horse. While I was doing that, Lay Me Down got up and walked across the pasture toward the barn. She looked normal for her, moving with choppy, stiff-kneed steps. What wasn't normal was her isolation from the herd and this delay in going to the barn at feed time.

I stood by one of the sections of hay and she came right over and sniffed it but didn't eat. I went back to the barn and brought out a bucket of grain and put it on the ground near the hay. She sniffed that, too, but didn't eat. Now what? I didn't know what to do, how to get through this day. For a second I felt panicky. Was she in pain? Nauseous? Suffering? Was waiting until two o'clock too long? How did you spend the last few hours with your horse?

I stood in front of her and started to cry. I dropped my chin onto my chest and let the tears roll down my face and onto my grimy blue sweatshirt. Then I sobbed, shoulder-shaking sobs that started in my stomach and felt like they'd split me open.

I couldn't bear that she was leaving me, that tomorrow morning she wouldn't be standing there. I wouldn't be able to touch her any longer. I couldn't bear it. I took a few steps toward her and leaned my forehead against her neck and wrapped my arms around her.

The last time we visited her in the hospital, you climbed into her bed, and it took two nurses to pull you away from her.

Lay Me Down didn't seem to mind my arms around her neck. When I stopped crying, I kept my head pressed against her. She was warm and alive.

I took a deep breath and picked up the bucket of grain. I took it back to the feed room and then let Hotshot out. Maybe without Georgia and Tempo around he'd go to be with Lay Me Down. And that's exactly what he did. As soon as I opened his stall door, he trotted right out, whinnying for her. When he saw her he went to her and sniffed her neck. She flicked her tail. He backed off a little and started eating hay. They were like an old married couple following their breakfast routine, only this morning the wife wasn't hungry. Still, at least she wasn't alone. I'd keep Georgia and Tempo inside, letting Lay Me Down and Hotshot have this day to themselves.

Two o'clock came fast. The hole was dug, Allie had come, and then Dr. Grice's blue truck pulled into the pasture right on time. I felt awful, jittery and sick and half out of my mind. I wondered if I could go through with it, if I could be present when Dr. Grice injected Lay Me Down. I could hardly talk to Allie. We'd been sitting on upturned buckets in the pasture watching Hotshot and Lay Me Down together while I fidgeted with a piece of baling twine.

"Let's get a halter on her," Allie said as Dr. Grice's truck pulled alongside the barn.

"I'll do it." I jumped up, glad for an excuse not to have to say hello to Dr. Grice. Allie could take care of the social amenities. I got Lay Me Down's halter and a lead line. My hands were jerky and clumsy. I dropped the halter, dropped the lead, kicked over the treat bucket. Stumbling around in the tack room, I realized there was nowhere to run, no way to escape dealing with this. If I ran all the way to China, Lay Me Down would still die. I'd still wake up tomorrow without her.

I heard the tack room door open.

It was Allie. "Bring Hotshot's halter, too," she said. "You have to put him in his stall until it's over."

Her voice was matter-of-fact. It was the voice of someone who had done this before, who knew what to do and what to expect. I didn't have a voice. Mine was the silence of fear. I was afraid of what would come out if I opened my mouth.

Outside I slipped Hotshot's halter on with shaky hands. I couldn't look at Dr. Grice. I couldn't even look at Hotshot. He followed me to his stall quietly but looked anxious when I shut his door and whinnied as I left the barn. I felt like a monster, as though I was killing him, too.

When I walked out of the barn I was assaulted by the sunshine. Allie was holding Lay Me Down by the halter while Dr. Grice listened to Lay Me Down's heart with a stethoscope. Dr. Grice's assistant, Donna, stood next to Allie with a stainless-steel pail. Inside the pail were two large syringes filled with blue liquid and a much smaller one filled with pink liquid.

Dr. Grice pulled the stethoscope out of her ears and turned to face me. "It's the right time," she said. "I'm glad it's warm and sunny for her."

I nodded, afraid if I opened my mouth I'd crack up.

Dr. Grice turned and talked to Lay Me Down. She stroked her neck, telling her she was a good horse, a wonderful horse. Allie talked to her, too, and so did Donna. I remained mute, silenced by my terror. The four of us surrounding Lay Me Down reminded me of Cornell; all those female vet students at Cornell, when there had still been hope.

After she had stroked Lay Me Down's neck, Dr. Grice explained what would happen. First would be the pink shot, a tranquilizer to relax Lay Me Down. Then we'd lead her to the hole, and she'd be given the blue lethal injection there. Usually one syringe was enough, but Dr. Grice had brought two, just in case. Most of the time the horse dropped fast. The drug went right to the heart; Lay Me Down wouldn't feel any pain.

She paused to see if I had any questions.

I shook my head.

"Shall we start?" she asked.

I nodded and walked over to hold Lay Me Down's halter. Dr. Grice took the syringe with the pink liquid and injected it into Lay Me Down's neck. In less than a minute Lay Me Down dropped her head and her eyes became sleepy.

"OK," Dr. Grice said. "Let's lead her to the hole."

On the way to the grave, I noticed Clayton's truck in the driveway. He was waiting until it was over, until it was time to *arrange her real pretty*.

When we got to the hole Dr. Grice handed me an apple. "Why don't you give her this while I inject her."

I stood right in front of Lay Me Down, who was noticeably drowsy from the tranquilizer. I hoped she felt fantastic. I hoped she felt loved. I pressed my lips against her forehead, only inches from the tumor, breathing in her horsey smell. "Thank you," I whispered. It was OK now. It was almost over.

I gave her the apple and felt the prickly whiskers of her chin in my palm. Before she had eaten half, she dropped straight down. I dropped next to her in the grass and held her beautiful head in my arms. It was heavy and warm against my chest. Her breath smelled like apple. She had fallen on her side, her long legs stretched away from her as though she was getting ready to roll, to take a lazy stretch in the afternoon sun. I looked down at the huge unmoving body and felt a moment of pure horror. What had we done? I wanted her to finish her apple, to have her get up. I wanted her back.

With trembling fingers I touched the silky ear, traced around the bony ridge of her temple, down her cheek to the curve of her jaw. It was a magnificent face, a marvel of contours. It was impossible to imagine where such beauty had come from, and now, where it would go. Allie knelt next to me in the grass, one hand stroking Lay Me Down's neck, the other around my shoulder. Dr. Grice knelt between Lay Me Down's outstretched legs, nestling her stethoscope high on her furry side to listen and confirm what we already knew.

"There's no heartbeat," she said a few minutes later, letting the stethoscope drop beside her in the grass. She stayed where she was, Donna next to her, still holding the pail with the extra syringe.

It was quiet in that back field, too far from the road to hear cars, too far from the barn to hear the swallows or the screeching of the killdeer nesting on rocks near the watering trough. We were quiet, too, the four of us, and it was in that silence, in the fragile warmth of the spring sun surrounded by gentleness and compassion that I stopped feeling afraid, that my heart stopped pounding and my hands stopped shaking.

I had lost love before, but even worse, I had lost the memory of love, all traces that it had ever existed. I wondered what I had left of Lay Me Down's love. What did I have to show for it, to prove that it had ever existed? With her head still warm in my arms, she already felt so far away, so very gone from me.

Allie, Dr. Grice, and Donna stayed where they were, kneeling in the grass. Somehow I understood that they weren't going to leave. They would stay for as long as I needed them to stay, absorbing this experience in their own way, but mostly they were there for me, to guide and support me through the death of my horse. No one was going to tell me to stop crying or to be strong or that I would be OK or that it was just a horse. No one was going to tell me how I should think or feel.

And it was in that gift of silence, that long beautiful pause, that I knew I could hold Lay Me Down's head for as long as I needed to, because no one who surrounded me now would ever pull me away.

[18]

A WEEK AFTER Lay Me Down died, Hank and I sat across the table from each other at a coffee shop in Kingston. It was noisy, filled with a noon lunch crowd. I ordered carrot soup. Hank ordered a Swiss cheese sandwich and a cup of herbal tea. While we waited for the food he sat perfectly still with his hands in his lap. I folded my paper napkin over and over until it was the size of a fat matchbook. I hated him.

"When were you going to tell me?" I asked.

He was wearing a navy T-shirt and khaki pants, more or less his uniform. He almost never wore a real shirt, not even when he flew to New York to put together the money, as he called it, for one of his malls. It struck me that there was an arrogance to his insistence on informality. He was the rich man who surprised you with his regular-guyness.

Imagine, he wanted people to say when he drove through town, *all that money, and he drives an old pickup*.

But that was only part of the message. The other part was a putdown of anyone's standard but his own. What he really wanted you to know, what I saw in his squared shoulders across the table, was that he was above explaining.

"I just met her," he said. "There's nothing to tell."

The waitress brought our food and smiled too much as she put it on the table. "Will there be anything else?" she chirped.

"No thanks." Hank smiled back. It made me angry that he could smile.

"If you tell me one more lie I'll throw this hot soup at you," I said when she left.

"Why don't we try to be sane about this." He sighed.

The white man's burden—an angry woman. "Why don't we try to be whatever we are."

He took big bites of his sandwich and crumbs fell all over his shirt and onto the table. I ignored my food and waited for him to say something. I wasn't sure what I wanted to hear, what he could possibly say that would take away my rage. I unfolded and refolded my napkin. I pictured carrot soup dripping off his head.

Finally he shrugged. "We don't want the same thing," he said. "I want to get married, to live with someone, and it's obvious you don't. Not with me."

That was true but beside the point. It wasn't his ending the relationship that bothered me, not entirely. It was the way he'd done it. In my mind, a relationship should end before either party began a new one. It was then that I knew what I wanted him to say. I wanted him to apologize, to say he was sorry for beginning a new relationship before he had ended ours. If he could say that, it would mean he hadn't lied about everything else. It would mean my feelings mattered.

"A woman in the grocery store told me," I said. "We were in produce. In front of all the lettuce." I could still see her hand fly to her mouth. I could still feel my wobbly knees.

He nodded and shrugged at the same time. As if to say, "*People,* if they would just mind their own business."

I hadn't touched my food and he had finished his. I saw him glance at my soup. "Go ahead," I said.

He pulled the bowl toward him and started on the soup. All he wanted was to eat. "I'm sorry," he said between spoonfuls. "I really did give it my best shot. Maybe if I'd been a horse." He looked up and smiled.

My shoulders dropped and I stopped mauling my napkin and let it fall on the table. He'd apologized. He'd even given a reason, a pretty good one. "If you hadn't been allergic," I said.

Our incompatibility was no one's fault. It was just there, huge and sad, a reminder that loneliness wasn't going to end yet. I'd have to look elsewhere, the way Hank already had. We'd been doomed from the start. I'd always known. Still, it felt so lousy to be forty-four and still getting it wrong, still going through these terrible endings, losing bits of myself each time.

I leaned back against the booth, suddenly too tired to feel angry anymore, too tired to hate him. It wasn't Hank I'd miss, or a warm body to hold, not really. What I missed was long gone, long before Hank. I couldn't blame him, I couldn't blame anyone for the stunning realization that I was no longer young, that I would never again be the "younger woman" with seemingly unlimited choices for love, for work, for a lifestyle. There was less time now, fewer selections at the buffet. The choicest portions were gone. A breathtaking fact—the passage of time. I was filled with sadness, with regrets for a misspent youth, a youth I had surely believed would go on forever.

I looked at Hank: the book hater, the mall builder, the horse avoider. Nothing so terrible, just terrible for me.

"I could go for something sweet," I said, watching a piece of blueberry pie go by on a tray.

I ordered the pie and when it arrived, Hank picked up his spoon and let it hover over my plate. "May I?"

I pulled the plate toward me, out of his reach, widening my eyes at him. "And risk a canker sore?"

AFTER LAY ME DOWN died, Hotshot whinnied for three days. He'd pull himself up from grazing suddenly and whinny straight into the sky, as if he knew how far away she was and he needed to give it everything he had in order for her to hear him.

The day Lay Me Down died, but before Clayton buried

her, Allie and I led the three horses over, one by one, to let them see her body. It was the humane thing to do, to let them know what had happened. Only Hotshot had reacted strongly. Georgia and Tempo had sniffed all around her with curiosity but without alarm. After a minute or two, both became more interested in the rich grass surrounding her than in her body.

Not Hotshot. When it was Hotshot's turn, just as I clipped on the lead to walk him over, he jerked away from me and started trotting toward Lay Me Down on his own, dragging his lead line on the ground. I ran after him, catching the end of the lead, but he wouldn't slow down, and I was dragged beside him into the back field. I never felt unsafe, as though he was going to hurt me. I only felt how strong he was, how impossible it was to control him, so out of character for this docile horse.

He dragged me into the field but stopped far short of Lay Me Down's body. He couldn't even see her. Thinking he was confused, unsure of where she actually was, I urged him forward in the direction of her body. As soon as he felt the pressure on his lead, though, his whole body went rigid, and he planted his front legs in a lock-kneed stop. His neck and head arched high above me, and, with a series of deep staccato grunts, his nostrils flared into the air as he swept the field for her scent.

His neck quivered at my touch, my presence clearly an intrusion. I didn't know what to do, how to ease his distress or unfreeze this moment. I was afraid he might gallop toward her, falling into the hole Clayton had dug. He seemed out of his mind, completely unhinged.

Before I could do anything, he started dragging me backward, at first backing up before whirling around and, this time, galloping toward the barn. I let him go. I couldn't have held on anyway. Allie saw him coming and once he was inside his own pasture, she ran and closed the gate behind him so he couldn't get out again. He circled the barn a few times, miraculously not tripping on his lead, and came to a stop at the gate he had just run through. If it had still been open, he would have run out again.

He stood wild-eyed and rigid, sending panicked whinnies in the direction of Lay Me Down. He let me approach to unclip his lead, but his neck quivered under my hand as though it burned him. There were sweat marks under his halter and down the inside of his legs.

His grief was beautiful and ferocious; his whole body shuddered with the thrust of each call. I stayed near him, close enough to feel his whinnies reverberate in my chest, as if they were mine. It was as if at last my grief, too, had the power to shake the ground and shatter the air between me and my beloved. It was as if my grief had finally found a memory, a voice. *It took two nurses to pull you away from her.* My mother's death was my death—a death and a birth at the same time. The death of the child I still only knew through my mother's eyes and the birth of someone unrecognizable—this new child, faceless without her mother mirror. A child with no proof of her own existence. The death of a mother is an annihilation of that first love, which is narcissistic and fierce by nature because survival hangs on it. Children understand commitment, the security of forever. They understand, too, the magnitude of its loss.

To love without an echo is the death knell of the soul. Foolishly, the soulless body grows anyway, marches into the future without its nucleus, without its self, bonsaied by this echoless love.

Hotshot's grief was big and bold, as unrestrained and open as his affection had been. Like mine. Lay Me Down had given us that, an echo. For me, it was the first I could remember feeling such love and then such grief, the first since the numbing years of childhood and then alcohol. Perhaps for Hotshot, as for me, Lay Me Down had been his first experience of pure kindness, of complete trust. She had loved us, she had loved me, and with that I had finally felt all the sorrow and joy that comes with it. I had learned something about courage, too, seeing her through her illness and even allowing a man into my life. Hank was the wrong man but it was a beginning, the first shaky steps. I would try again. There was no going back.

Allie and I left and Clayton buried her. I couldn't bear to watch this final step, to see her shoveled into the hole with a backhoe and *arranged real pretty* in the dirt. When he had finished and her grave was tamped flat, he used the bucket loader to scoop up a rock from the stone wall to use as a grave marker. The rock was large and flat, covered with curly green lichen. It would be a good place to sit on a summer evening, listening to the peepers and tree frogs.

Late in the summer when I was harvesting some leeks from the garden, I realized they were from Lay Me Down. They *were* Lay Me Down, grown in her composted manure along with Hotshot's and Tempo's and Georgia's, but most joyously, Lay Me Down's.

I drove to Allie's house with the sacred leeks and laid them on her kitchen counter, four long stalks smelling of earth and onion. I started imagining all the ways Lay Me Down would come back to me: as leeks, as wild roses climbing along the stone wall, as the baby cedar growing next to her grave, as clover and timothy.

"We have to make something with these," I said. I explained about the leeks, about how they were actually Lay Me Down.

Allie didn't laugh. She didn't inform me as to whether the leeks contained Lay Me Down's DNA or not. She didn't say horses can't make cold, shut-down people into loving, open ones. She didn't say horses can't save us. She didn't say anything. She put her arms around me and held me for a moment and then put some water on the stove to make us tea.

Acknowledgments

Heartfelt thanks to my wise and beautiful agent, Helen Zimmermann, who made a dream come true. Much admiration, praise, and thanks to my wonderful editors: Laura Hruska, Nan Satter, and Patricia Sims. To my friends for their unwavering support and love: Elaine Ralston, Patti Reller, Sara Beames, Dorothy Porter, Daia Gerson, Nancy April, Pat Whelan, John McCauley, Stephanie Speer, Alex Rambusch, and Barbara Scanlan. And much love and gratitude to my brother, Lloyd, the writer of a thousand encouraging, funny, and nourishing e-mails.